CAMBRIDGE TEXTS IN THE
HISTORY OF PHILOSOPHY

———

ARTHUR SCHOPENHAUER
Prize Essay on the Freedom of the Will

CAMBRIDGE TEXTS IN THE
HISTORY OF PHILOSOPHY

Series editors

KARL AMERIKS
Professor of Philosophy, University of Notre Dame

DESMOND M. CLARKE
Professor of Philosophy, University College Cork

The main objective of Cambridge Texts in the History of Philosophy is to expand the range, variety and quality of texts in the history of philosophy which are available in English. The series includes texts by familiar names (such as Descartes and Kant) and also by less well-known authors. Wherever possible, texts are published in complete and unabridged form, and translations are specially commissioned for the series. Each volume contains a critical introduction together with a guide to further reading and any necessary glossaries and textual apparatus. The volumes are designed for student use at undergraduate and postgraduate level and will be of interest not only to students of philosophy but also to a wider audience of readers in the history of science, the history of theology and the history of ideas.

For a list of titles published in the series, please see end of book.

ARTHUR SCHOPENHAUER

Prize Essay on the Freedom of the Will

EDITED BY

GÜNTER ZÖLLER

University of Iowa

TRANSLATED BY

ERIC F. J. PAYNE

CAMBRIDGE
UNIVERSITY PRESS

PUBLISHED BY THE PRESS SYNDICATE OF THE UNIVERSITY OF CAMBRIDGE
The Pitt Building, Trumpington Street, Cambridge CB2 1RP, United Kingdom

CAMBRIDGE UNIVERSITY PRESS
The Edinburgh Building, Cambridge, CB2 2RU, United Kingdom   http://www.cup.cam.ac.uk
40 West 20th Street, New York, NY 10011-4211, USA   http://www.cup.org
10 Stamford Road, Oakleigh, Melbourne 3166, Australia

First published 1999

Printed in the United Kingdom at the University Press, Cambridge

Typeset in 11/13 Ehrhardt   [CP]

A catalogue record for this book is available from the British Library

Library of Congress cataloguing in publication data
Schopenhauer, Arthur, 1788–1860.
[Preisschrift über die Freiheit des Willens. English]
Prize essay on the freedom of the will / Arthur Schopenhauer:
edited by Günter Zöller; translated by Eric F. J. Payne.
p.   cm. – (Cambridge texts in the history of philosophy)
Includes index.
ISBN 0 521 57141 3 (hardback) – ISBN 0 521 57766 7 (paperback)
1. Free will and determinism.
I. Zöller, Günter, 1954–   . II. Title. III. Series.
B3144.U352E5   1999
123´.5–dc21   98–22360 CIP

ISBN 0 521 57141 3 hardback
ISBN 0 521 57766 7 paperback

Contents

Acknowledgments   *page* vii
Introduction   ix
Chronology   xxx
Further reading   xxxiii
Note on the text and translation   xxxv

Prize Essay on the Freedom of the Will   I
  I   Definitions   3
  II   The will before self-consciousness   12
  III   The will before the consciousness of other things   23
  IV   Predecessors   56
  V   Conclusion and higher view   81
  Appendix, supplementing the first section   89

Appendix: Eric F. J. Payne, translator   93
BRYAN MAGEE

Index   97

v

Acknowledgments

The plan for this edition goes back to conversations about Schopen-hauer with Bryan Magee in the common room at Wolfson College, Oxford, in the latter part of Hilary term 1994. In the course of our discussions I brought up the fact that the *Prize Essay on the Freedom of the Will* was missing from the extensive list of Schopenhauer transla-tions published by the late Eric Payne, the main English translator of Schopenhauer in the twentieth century. I ventured the theory that Payne had undertaken the translation of the *Prize Essay* but failed to publish it after another translation of the work appeared in 1960. Bryan Magee, who had known Eric Payne, agreed to contact Payne's grandson and heir, Christophe Egret, in an effort to search for the missing translation among Payne's literary remains. Several months after my return to the States, the typescript with Payne's complete translation of Schopenhauer's *Prize Essay* arrived in the mail. Karl Ameriks took an interest in the work, kindly agreed to publish it in the series Cambridge Texts in the History of Philosophy, and provided valuable editorial advice. Christophe Egret graciously granted permission to use the translation. Bryan Magee gladly contributed a note on Eric Payne. I am most grateful to Bryan Magee, Christophe Egret, and Karl Ameriks for their support of this project, and to Hilary Gaskin for seeing it through to publication. Further thanks go to the fellows of Queen's College, Oxford, and especially Susanne Bobzien for making me an additional member of Common Room at Queen's in 1994. Special thanks are due to my wife and colleague, Marlena Corcoran, for introducing me to Bryan Magee, her fellow visiting fellow at Wolfson at the time.

In 1996 the University of Iowa Libraries acquired Eric Payne's literary remains along with the rights to their use for research and publication. Edward Shreeves, Director of Collections and Information Resources, University of Iowa Libraries, granted permission to use Payne's translation of the *Prize Essay* for the present edition.

I gratefully acknowledge support for my stay at Oxford in the form of a Fellowship for University Teachers from the National Endowment for the Humanities in 1993–94 and additional funds from the University of Iowa, and support for my work on the edition from the Obermann Center for Advanced Studies at the University of Iowa. Maurene Morgan from the staff of the Department of Philosophy at the University of Iowa provided valuable secretarial help. My doctoral student, Claudia Schmidt, made helpful suggestions on the entire manuscript. In her research on the English names of three plants incidentally mentioned by Schopenhauer she was aided by Leo Clougherty and Barbara Brodersen from the Chemistry/Botany Library at the University of Iowa.

Introduction

In April 1837 the Royal Norwegian Society of Sciences announced the following prize question in a German literary journal:

> Can the freedom of the will be proven from self-consciousness?

The entry for which the prize, a gold medal, was awarded in 1839 had been submitted by one Arthur Schopenhauer, a fifty-two-year-old German private scholar residing in Frankfurt-on-Main, for whom this was his first public recognition as a philosopher. None of Schopenhauer's earlier publications, including the first edition of his main work, *The World as Will and Representation* (1818),[1] had attracted any attention in the world of academic philosophy, and it was not until some fifteen years after the *Prize Essay* and then in the decades after his death in 1860 that Schopenhauer became recognized and admired as the leading philosophical voice of the time.

Given the conditions of anonymity under which the *Prize Essay* had to be submitted to the Society, Schopenhauer was not able to refer explicitly and specifically to his previously published views on the matter. As a result, the *Prize Essay on the Freedom of the Will* is a freestanding piece of philosophy, and one of the more lucid and penetrating examinations of the topic, at that. The independent and self-sufficient status of the work is further due to Schopenhauer's estrangement from the academic philosophy of his day. At a time when the idealist metaphysics of Georg Wilhelm Friedrich Hegel (1770–1831) and his followers, with its detailed knowledge claims

[1] Trans. Eric F. J. Payne, 2 vols. (New York: Dover, 1974). Vol. I corresponds to the first edition of the work.

about the absolute or God, dominated the teaching of philosophy at German universities, Schopenhauer upheld the critical standards for any possible metaphysics introduced by Immanuel Kant (1724–1804) in the *Critique of Pure Reason* (1781; second, revised edition 1787)[2] and the *Prolegomena to Any Future Metaphysics* (1783).[3] It was not until the mid nineteenth century that German academic philosophy, in a movement which came to be known as neo-Kantianism,[4] returned to its roots in Kant, to which Schopenhauer had stayed close all along.

To be sure, even Schopenhauer's allegiance to Kant was selective and revisionist. Most notably, he rejected the categorical imperative as the principle of morality, replacing the command to act on a principle of action that can be consistently willed by everyone with an ethics of compassion built on the recognition of the ultimate identity of doer and sufferer.[5] Most important, Schopenhauer identified Kant's "thing in itself," that unknown and unknowable reality behind the spatiotemporal order of things, with the will, understood to include striving of all kinds in all kinds of beings.[6] But Schopenhauer's metaphysics of the will is virtually absent from the *Prize Essay*, as is his critique of Kant's ethics. In fact, the work can be regarded as a systematic presentation of the Kantian position on the matter and as such could have been written half a century earlier, were it not for the polemical asides on the development of philosophy since Kant.

A sketch of Schopenhauer's life

Schopenhauer's position as an outsider in academic life in general and university philosophy in particular is rooted in his life story as a gentleman scholar of independent means and an equally independent mind. Born on 22 February 1788 in the free city of Danzig (today's

---

[2] Trans. Paul Guyer and Allen Wood (Cambridge: Cambridge University Press, 1998). The *Critique of Pure Reason* will be cited after the pagination of the first and second editions ("A" and "B," respectively) indicated in the standard modern editions and translations of the work.

[3] Trans. Gary Hatfield (Cambridge: Cambridge University Press, 1997). The *Prolegomena* will be cited after the pagination of the work in vol. IV of the Academy edition (*Kant's gesammelte Schriften*, ed. Royal Prussian Academy of Sciences and its successors [Berlin: Reimer, later de Gruyter, 1900ff.]) indicated in the standard modern editions and translations of the work.

[4] See Klaus Christian Köhnke, *The Rise and Fall of Neo-Kantianism: German Academic Philosophy Between Idealism and Positivism* (Cambridge: Cambridge University Press, 1991).

[5] See Arthur Schopenhauer, *On the Basis of Morality*, trans. Eric F. J. Payne. rev. ed. with an introduction by David E. Cartwright (Providence, RI and Oxford: Berghahn, 1995).

[6] See *The World as Will and Representation*, vol. I, 93ff.

Gdansk in Poland) into a wealthy Hanseatic merchant family and destined to be the future head of the family firm, Schopenhauer was free to pursue his scholarly interests only after his father's sudden death in 1805 (probably by suicide). He studied sciences and philosophy at the University of Göttingen (1809–11) and the University of Berlin (1811–13) and received his doctorate *in absentia* from the University of Jena in 1813. The main influences on his philosophical outlook were Plato and Kant, and, later, Hindu and Buddhist thought, which he was the first European philosopher to incorporate in his philosophical work. Another formative influence was Johann Wolfgang Goethe (1749–1832), whom he met in the literary salon of his mother, Johanna Schopenhauer, in Weimar. Schopenhauer was only thirty when he published his main philosophical work, which was the first completely elaborated system of philosophy to appear since Kant.[7]

Schopenhauer spent the next four decades supplementing and expanding it in monographs and essay collections. Throughout his life he kept up with the latest scientific developments, especially in physiology, as well as with political events at home and abroad. Although nominally affiliated with the University of Berlin as an unsalaried lecturer from 1819 until 1831, he conducted a lecture course only once (1820). Schopenhauer traveled extensively throughout Europe, living in France, England, and Italy for extended periods of time and finally settling in Frankfurt-on-Main in 1833, where he died on 21 September 1860. His influence reaches from Richard Wagner and Friedrich Nietzsche through Sigmund Freud and Ludwig Wittgenstein to Samuel Beckett. He remains one of the finest writers of German prose.

The organization of the *Prize Essay*

The *Prize Essay* is in five sections. The first section defines the key concepts referred to in the Society's question, viz., freedom and self-consciousness. The second section provides an answer in the negative to the question posed: it is impossible to prove the freedom of the will from self-consciousness. The third section widens the basis of the

---

[7] The two further competitors for the title of first complete philosophical system since Kant, Schelling's *System of Transcendental Idealism* from 1800 and Hegel's *Encyclopedia of the Philosophical Sciences in Outline* from 1817, are more schemas of a complete philosophical system than actual, specific, and detailed executions of such a system.

investigation by turning to a possible alternative source of evidence for the freedom of the will, viz., the consciousness of other things. But again the answer is negative: it is impossible to prove the freedom of the will from the consciousness of other objects. Moreover, in principle there can be no instance of freedom of the will anywhere in the sphere of experience. In the fourth section Schopenhauer presents philosophical, theological, and literary predecessors who held or defended the view that there is no freedom of the will. The short fifth section provides a last-minute dramatic reversal of the situation by appealing to the phenomenon of moral responsibility as evidence for the freedom of the will and by introducing a "higher view" from which the freedom of the will can be maintained although not explained or understood. The essay concludes with an appendix supplementing the definitional considerations of freedom in section I.

One might regard Schopenhauer's treatment of the freedom of the will as a rigorous and successful defense of determinism, the position that everything in experience is completely determined as to the time and place of its occurrence. The final rescue effort on behalf of the will's freedom might then be dismissed as inconsistent with the main parts of the work and to be eliminated from consideration in the text. But such a selective appropriation of the *Prize Essay* as a canonical defense of determinism would not only be incomplete but would also overlook the preparation for the dramatic finale in the preceding sections of the work. Far from being a relapse into a previously overcome position, the concluding defense of freedom is the well-prepared culmination of the *Prize Essay.*

Physical, intellectual, and moral freedom

For Schopenhauer, freedom is a *negative* concept that indicates the absence of hindrances to the exercise of some force. Depending on the nature of the force that is subject to or free from hindrances, three kinds of freedom are to be distinguished. *Physical freedom* is the absence of *material* hindrances in the exercise of some *physical force.* *Intellectual freedom* is the absence of *intellectual* impairment in some *cognitive force* or in cognition. *Moral freedom* is the absence of *motivational* hindrances in some *volitional force* or in willing.

Each of the three forms of freedom bears a relation to the will. The physical freedom of the will consists in its ability to be exercised free of external, physical constraints. Intellectual freedom is the will's freedom from cognitive error. Moral freedom is the freedom of the will from motivational constraints, historically expressed in the Latin term *liberum arbitrium* or "free choice of the will." It is the third kind of freedom, moral freedom, that is at issue in the *Prize Essay*.

After consigning the discussion of intellectual freedom to the appendix, Schopenhauer clarifies further the conceptual difference between physical and moral freedom. It is important to realize that the terminological contrast between the two kinds of freedom does not concern the specific opposition between nature and morality but refers to the more general distinction between the physical domain and the psychical or mental domain. The wider sense of "moral" that is operative here underlies, e.g., the older designation of the humanities as the "moral sciences."

Physical freedom is defined as the ability to act in accordance with one's will in the absence of external hindrances. Freedom so defined does not concern the question whether the will itself might be constrained but involves only the relation between a given will and the action willed and carried out under conditions of physical freedom. Schopenhauer sees no problem in asserting the reality of freedom in the physical sense. In fact, in line with popular linguistic practice, he even extends the application of the concept to include not only human, rational animals but animal beings in general and applies it as well to collective entities such as nations or peoples.

In the case of moral freedom, the concept of freedom no longer concerns the freedom to do as one wills, but the freedom of willing or that of the will itself. The question is no longer whether one can *do* what one *wills*, but whether – in Schopenhauer's own intentionally paradoxical formulation – one can *will* what one wills. Formulated this way, the question suggests the possible dependence of one's overt, manifest will on some hidden prior will, and so on *ad infinitum*. Schopenhauer's point here is that the ordinary, popular thinking about freedom, as codified in the physical sense of the term, is ill suited to posing the question of the moral freedom of the will.

In order to address more adequately the sense in which the will itself and as such might be free, Schopenhauer turns to an alternative generic definition of freedom, again a negative one, viz., the absence of *necessity*, and proceeds to define the underlying positive conception of necessity. Necessary is what follows from a given sufficient reason or ground.[8] Schopenhauer regards necessity and consequence from a sufficient ground or reason as reciprocal concepts that define each other. Something is the sufficient reason for something else if and only if the former and the latter are related with necessity as ground and consequent.

Schopenhauer had devoted his doctoral dissertation of 1813 to a systematic study of the principle of sufficient reason. The dissertation, first published in 1814 and later revised (1841) in light of his main work, to which it serves as an introduction of sorts, has remained the classic treatment of the principle.[9] In the *Prize Essay* Schopenhauer recapitulates the main points of the earlier work.

Schopenhauer distinguishes three kinds of reason and, accordingly, three kinds of necessity, to which he will later add a fourth kind of ground and necessity pertinent to the human will. First, there is reason in the *logical* sense, and the associated logical necessity, which obtains, e.g., between the premise or premises of an argument and the conclusion. If the premises are given, the conclusion necessarily follows.

Second, there is the *mathematical* sense of reason and the allied mathematical necessity, exemplified by the equality of the sides in a triangle with equal angles. Given the equality of the angles, equilaterality necessarily obtains.

Third, there is the *physical* sense of reason and its peculiar physical necessity, which holds between cause and effect in the physical world. The effect occurs as soon as the cause is given. Schopenhauer regards the law of causality, according to which every event in the physical world has a cause from which it follows necessarily, as one of several manifestations of the general principle of sufficient reason that is said to govern thinking about objects of all kinds – logical and mathematical as well as physical objects.

Given the notion of necessity as consequence from a given sufficient reason, freedom understood as the absence of necessity would consist in

---

[8] Schopenhauer follows the customary German translation of the Latin term "principium rationis sufficientis," rendered in English as "principle of sufficient reason," by employing the German term for "ground" (*Grund*) for the Latin "ratio" (*Satz vom zureichenden Grund*).

[9] English translation of the second, revised edition as *On the Fourfold Root of the Principle of Sufficient Reason*, trans. Eric F. J. Payne (La Salle, IL: Open Court, 1974). See also F. C. White, *On Schopenhauer's "Fourfold Root of the Principle of Sufficient Reason"* (Leiden: Brill, 1992).

the lack of any sufficient reason and hence in utter contingency. The only realm in which there is contingency is the real or physical world. Therefore the ideal worlds of logic and mathematics remain out of consideration in Schopenhauer's further discussion of freedom, necessity, and contingency.

Now it is indeed the case that in the physical world an event is necessary only in relation to its own sufficient cause while being contingent with respect to all other circumstances. But nothing in the physical world is entirely contingent and not necessary with regard to anything. Yet to claim that something is free is to claim that it lacks necessity in each and every regard, and hence is entirely contingent. The free can be defined as that which is absolutely contingent.

Applied to the case of the human will, freedom as absolute contingency would consist in the fact that a particular act of volition is not determined by any sufficient reason in general and any cause in particular. But the very notion of an absolutely undetermined will or act of will is unintelligible. All human thinking follows the principle of sufficient reason in one of its specifically different forms. Still, there is a technical term for an absolutely undetermined will, viz., *liberum arbitrium indifferentiae* (free choice of indifference). The term implies that to a given individual under specifically determined circumstances two diametrically opposed actions are equally possible. Schopenhauer will return to this issue after defining self-consciousness and introducing the peculiar kind of necessity involved in human volition.

Defining self-consciousness

Schopenhauer distinguishes two kinds of consciousness or awareness: the consciousness of one's own self and the consciousness of other things, including other selves. He further identifies the latter with the faculty of cognition. Even the universal forms and conditions of all cognition, which – with Kant – he takes to be subjective in nature and identifies as space, time, and causality, are said to belong to the consciousness of other things rather than to self-consciousness. For Schopenhauer consciousness is primarily and for the most part directed toward the real world outside us, standing to it in the relation of apprehension and comprehension.

By contrast, self-consciousness is for Schopenhauer the immediate awareness of one's own *willing*. Self-consciousness is the consciousness of oneself as willing. The notion of willing employed here covers the whole range of a person's affective inner life, not just the resulting actual decisions and actions. In addition to the overtly volitional activities, it also includes the feelings of pleasure and displeasure. Schopenhauer is here effectively regrouping the faculty of desire and the feeling of pleasure and displeasure, which Kant had treated in strict separation in his *Critique of Practical Reason* (1788)[10] and *Critique of Judgment* (1790),[11] respectively, under the comprehensive heading of will, willing, or volition.

Whereas the sole object of self-consciousness as such is the ceaseless coming and going of positive or pleasurable and negative or displeasurable affections, the objects of the will's affective responses are provided by the outside world mediated through the faculty of cognition in the consciousness of objects. But any consideration of the will's dependence on the consciousness of other things already falls outside the narrow sphere of self-consciousness as such. It is that confined sphere which has to be examined for evidence of the will's freedom.

Wishing and willing

On Schopenhauer's analysis, the act of willing that forms the immediate object of self-consciousness occurs on the occasion of some instance of consciousness of other things. In fact, willing is nothing but the affective and appetitive reaction to a given external cognition. Schopenhauer terms the cognition insofar as it sets the will in motion the "motive." The question concerning the freedom of the will now takes the following form: whether the will – more precisely, the given particular act of the will or volition – is necessitated by the given motive, or whether, the given motive notwithstanding, the volitional act in question might not occur or some other volition might occur. Given the terms set by the Society, that question has to be answered on the basis of the data to be found in immediate self-consciousness.

But self-consciousness proves to be singularly ill equipped to address,

---

[10] Trans. Mary Gregor, in Immanuel Kant, *Practical Philosophy*, trans. and ed. Mary Gregor (Cambridge: Cambridge University Press, 1996). The *Critique of Practical Reason* is cited after the pagination of the work in vol. v of the Academy edition indicated in the standard modern editions and translations of the work.

[11] Trans. Werner Pluhar (Indianapolis: Hackett, 1995).

much less answer, the question of the will's freedom. All that can be established on the basis of self-consciousness as such is that in any number of instances one can do what one wills, as evidenced by the immediate manifestations of one's willing in one's bodily activity. But this ability to act in accordance with the will is none other than the *physical* freedom already discussed and dismissed as beside the point to be established, viz., the (moral) freedom of willing that might, or might not, underlie the (physical) freedom of acting.

The insufficiency of the data provided by self-consciousness for determining whether the will is free is due to that faculty's structural limitations. The question of the will's freedom concerns the nature of the relation between motives, originating in the external world as perceived and comprehended by the human mind, and acts of volition, occurring in one's inner, affective world. But self-consciousness as such is limited to the latter and cannot provide any basis for judging the motivational force of some cognition on the very formation of the volition.

In the perspective of self-consciousness, desires and intentions arise and interact in various ways. But this multifarious and often contradictory *wishing* must not be confused with the eventual *willing* that replaces the previously entertained possible and possibly competing actions with the one deed actually willed and immediately carried out through bodily movement. There is no way to know the prevailing desire or intention before the decisive act of the will and its bodily manifestation have occurred. Much less is there any evidence available in self-consciousness about the circumstances of the will's decision process.

Schopenhauer attributes the widespread belief in the freedom of the will to the inability of the ordinary mind to distinguish between the statement that one is free to *think* or *consider* oneself willing any one of a number of contrary things, on the one hand, and the statement that one is free to *will* any one of a number of contrary things, on the other hand. The former statement is true; the latter statement requires further investigation, given the insufficient evidence provided by self-consciousness.

At this point the specific question of the Society about the evidential basis in self-consciousness for the freedom of the will has been answered in the negative. Schopenhauer proposes to continue the inquiry with the aim of complementing the previous direct and specific investigation of the actuality of freedom based on the data of self-consciousness with the indirect and more general investigation of the very possibility of a free will. If the impossibility of the will's freedom could be established independent of the inconclusive evidence of self-consciousness on the matter, then this would confirm in principle what has already been established on limited, empirical grounds. There can be no evidence of something that is not even possible in the first place.

Motivational causation

The alternative source of evidence to which Schopenhauer turns is the faculty of cognition. So far the will has been considered *subjectively* or from within one's own experience of willing. Henceforth the will is considered *objectively*, in the external perspective of an outside observer and examiner who seeks to ascertain the precise relation between motivational consciousness of objects and motivated will. The inquiry moves from the will as the immediate object of self-consciousness to the will as the mediate object of the consciousness of objects. In the new perspective the will comes into view as a faculty possessed by a being that exists in the physical world.

As part of an entity in the physical world, the will is subject to the principles and laws of nature, chief among them the law of causality. On Schopenhauer's view, the law of causality as one of the specific forms that the principle of sufficient reason takes invariably informs the experience of any being endowed with an understanding or intellect. In addition to governing the perception and conception of the physical world, the law of causality is also the basic law of the physical world so perceived and conceived. Schopenhauer here follows Kant's identification of the necessary conditions of experience on the part of a *subject* with the necessary conditions of the *objects* of that subject's experience.[12] Under the law of causality, all changes in the physical world have their sufficient reason or cause. Nothing happens without cause; and given its cause, it happens necessarily. The law holds strictly, without exception; everything in the real world that undergoes change is subject to it.

---

[12] See *Critique of Pure Reason*, A 111; *Prolegomena*, Academy edition, IV, 296.

In order to ascertain what might be specific to the operation of the law of causality in the case of a being endowed with a will, Schopenhauer adopts the familiar classification of beings as lifeless or inorganic and living or organic, and further distinguishes between vegetative or plant life and animal life. In inorganic beings the specific causal relation obtains between a mechanical, physical, or chemical *cause* (or a cause in the narrow sense) and some such effect. In plants the specific causal relation holds between *stimulus*, such as water, air, and heat, and response, such as growth. In animals the specific causal relation takes the form of *motivation* understood as causality operating by means of cognition bringing about a willed action.

Schopenhauer offers an evolutionary account of the emergence and development of the cognitive and conative abilities of animal life. The increased organizational complexity of higher life forms brings with it a manifold of needs that can no longer be adequately satisfied on the basis of stimulus and response. In addition, there is now the animal's susceptibility to motives or its capacity to be moved by the representation of objects, i.e., by cognition. Schopenhauer attributes the capacity to represent relevant aspects of the world to *all* animals but notes the increase in cognitive abilities in correlation with the development of their physiological basis in the nervous system and the brain. Moreover, he identifies the animal's ability to act upon motives as *will*.

In nonrational animals the faculty of cognition is limited to the *perception* of what is immediately given. Nonrational cognition consists in the *intuitive* apprehension of the external world. For Schopenhauer the intuition of the spatiotemporal world already involves some operation of the intellect or understanding, which assigns to given sensations by means of the instinctually employed principle of causality a world of objects impinging upon the animal. In rational animals or human beings the faculty of cognition also includes reason, which is the ability to form universal concepts that transcend the specifics of a given situation. Once formed, the concepts are designated by words and used in all manners of combination, thereby adding to the perception of the external world through *intuition* its grasp through concepts introduced by the activity of *thought*.

Owing to reason or the rational faculty of cognition, the human being is susceptible to motives that are not directly given in perception but are present in the medium of thought. Moreover, the human being is able to exercise a measure of control over the motives that take the form of thoughts. Such motives can be compared and weighed against each other in acts of *deliberation*. Accordingly, rational animals exercise a much higher degree of choice in their volitional processes than nonrational animals. One may even speak of the *relative or comparative freedom* which human beings possess: they are free from the immediate compulsion through the intuitive, nonconceptual motives and hence free by comparison with their nonrational fellow animals.

But on closer inspection it becomes clear that the conceptually mediated motive is just as much a cause as the strictly perceptual motive. Freedom of deliberation is not freedom from motivation. In rational deliberation human consciousness becomes the battleground for conflicting motives, each of which seeks to influence the will. Finally, one motive prevails over the others and succeeds in determining the will. This is the moment of decision, which occurs by no means freely but in strict necessity, caused by the victorious motive.

In essence, the causal efficacy of motivation to be found in a being endowed with a will, or an animal, is no different from the causal necessity involved in the two lower forms of causality specific to inorganic matter and plants, respectively. In each case, some change is brought about with necessity, given a sufficient reason or cause. What is specifically different about motivational causation in general and rational motivational causation in particular is (1) the heterogeneity between the immaterial, merely mental cause and its physical effect of bodily motion, and (2) the fact that in motivation causality is no longer only externally observed, and perhaps measured, but actually experienced from within in its effect on the will. But this changes nothing in the causal necessitation of the will by the prevailing motive. Schopenhauer acknowledges the peculiarity of volitional or motivational causation by introducing it as a fourth form of the principle of sufficient reason.

Schopenhauer argues that a human being can just as little get up from a chair without a motive that compels him or her to do so than a billiard ball can move on a table before receiving a push. The human being is considered here as an object of experience subject to the same basic principle (the law of causality) as anything else to be encountered in space and time. To maintain the freedom of the human will would turn each and every human action into an "inexplicable miracle" by introducing effects without cause.

Motive and character

In further explaining the operation of causality in empirical objects in general and human beings in particular, Schopenhauer distinguishes two factors that jointly bring about the effect: (1) an original *force* inherent in the object on which the causal influence is being exercised and (2) a determining *cause* that makes the force manifest itself. Thus causal efficacy always requires some force, and any causal explanation needs to have recourse to some such force. Moreover, the force itself lies outside the domain of the relation between cause and effect; it underlies all causal relation but is not subject to it.

On Schopenhauer's account of causality, the cause provides the occasion on which the force produces the effect. All causes are occasioning causes, and that out of which the effect proceeds is not the cause but the force. Forces in Schopenhauer take on the role of powers or capacities in earlier accounts of causation, such as Aristotle's. Yet for Schopenhauer the recourse to forces is not sufficient to explain the necessity of physical change. Forces as potentialities need to be subject to specific conditions in order to actualize themselves in specific ways. Those conditions are provided by the causes.

With the introduction of forces as involved in all causality but neither caused nor causing, there emerges something nonphysical, even metaphysical, at the very core of physical reality in Schopenhauer. It is this metaphysical core of the physical that will provide the basis for Schopenhauer's concluding reintroduction of freedom.

Schopenhauer distinguishes several classes of forces in accordance with his classification of causes. Examples of forces behind causes in the narrow sense are electricity and magnetism. The force behind the physiological causality operative in living beings is termed "life force." Finally, the force that is specific to animals is none other than the will. In each case, Schopenhauer stresses the inexplicable, unfathomable character of the original force. The original forces cannot be reduced to each other or to something else. They mark the end points of all inquiry. All that can be ascertained about original forces are the lawful conditions for their specific actualizations. This is exactly the business of the natural sciences.

Schopenhauer's closer examination of the force peculiar to animals in general and rational animals or human beings in particular is concerned with the specific quality of the will due to which the same motive may result in different reactions in different animal species and in different human beings, respectively. Schopenhauer terms this peculiarity the *character* of the being or beings in question. While animal character varies from species to species, human character varies from one individual to the other. Character is the property of the motivational force (will) of a being to react specifically or individually to motives. Schopenhauer thinks of a being's character as the core or very essence of that being.

Schopenhauer lists four main features of the character of human beings. They are not individual character traits but traits of human character as such. The human character is (1) individual, (2) empirical, (3) constant, and (4) inborn.

Whereas there is an underlying character of the human species as such, each individual of the species exhibits its own character. This accounts for the fact that the effect of the same motive (cognition) on different human individuals is quite different.

The human character is, moreover, nothing that can be ascertained prior to its exercise in particular acts of volition. Each individual human being discovers its own character as well as that of its fellow human beings only through experience, hence over time. Furthermore, the empirically acquired knowledge of one's own individual character informs one's future decisions and plans, thus resulting in a secondary or *acquired character* that reflects the possibilities as well as limitations of one's basic, inborn character. The acquired character is like the role that the individual develops for itself in response to its basic character. But the acquisition of secondary character traits can never alter the basic character itself, which remains unchanged or constant over an individual's entire lifetime. Any appearance of change in someone's character should be regarded as evidence that the character was different to begin with and had been misconstrued previously. Schopenhauer claims that in effect each and every one operates on the assumption of the constancy of the human character.

Although it is not possible to change an individual's basic character,

Schopenhauer believes it possible to either reinforce or discourage the manifestations of the character. This can be managed by appealing to the individual's intellect or understanding, providing the latter either with powerful motives or with strong countermotives for certain actions.

Finally, the individual character is already wholly formed at the moment of birth and is not the result of any subsequent natural or cultural influences. Schopenhauer asserts that virtues as well as vices are inborn and not the result of some later acquisition. The constant and inborn nature of human individual character rules out the possibility that an individual in a given situation is free to choose among two or more possible courses of action. The character together with the motive or motives present in the situation determines the individual's course of action unfailingly. For a different action to occur, the motive or the character would have had to be different.

Schopenhauer summarizes his account of necessary change in natural beings of all kinds by resorting to the scholastic formula "acting follows being" (*operari sequitur esse*). Any action, whether physical, chemical, vegetative, sensible, or rational, follows from the being of the entity in question. "Being" here includes not only *existence* – *that* something is – but also essence – *what* it is. To be sure, it is not just anything in and about an existent, such as an actual human being, that counts as its essence but only that entity's basic nature, i.e., its character.

Schopenhauer claims that the strict necessity of all events has been felt, if not properly understood, for a long time in many cultures and by numerous individuals. He mentions specifically the religious conception of fate in classical antiquity, the fatalism of the Islamic faith, and the Christian doctrine of predestination.

In the section of the *Prize Essay* devoted to identifying individual predecessors for the determinist conception of the human will, Schopenhauer cites not only religious authorities, among them Saint Augustine and Martin Luther, and philosophers, including Hobbes, Spinoza, Hume, Priestley, Voltaire, Kant, and Schelling, but also the dramatic poets and novelists Shakespeare, Sir Walter Scott, Goethe, and Schiller. The point of naming these predecessors is not to mount an argument from authority that would supplement the earlier argument from reason or to document a record of widespread consensus on the matter.

On the contrary, Schopenhauer firmly believes in the prevalence of error among his fellow human beings. True insight into the operations of the human will is the prerogative of the few. The particular assertion which the section on predecessors is designed to support is that of universal agreement on the will's unfreedom among "true thinkers."

Idealism to the rescue

For Schopenhauer the problem of the freedom of the will is one of the two problems that have most deeply occupied modern European philosophy since Descartes, the other being the problem of the relation between thought and reality. The two basic problems of modern philosophy are moreover structurally related in that each of them concerns the relation between the subject and the object. In one case, it is the epistemic relation between the subject of knowledge and the object known, addressed in modern epistemology; in the other case, it is the practical relation between the subject of willing and the object willed, as examined by modern moral philosophy.

Schopenhauer notes that the ordinary understanding is prone to opposite errors in the assessment of the two basic relations between subject and object. With respect to the epistemic relation, the untutored mind tends to attribute too much to the side of the object and too little to the side of the subject. The work of Locke[13] and Kant on the cognitive functions of the mind can be seen as attempts at correcting this popular misconception of what is involved in knowing. Both Locke and Kant demonstrate how much of our knowledge concerning objects originates in the knowing subject. By contrast, in regard to the practical relation, the untutored mind tends to attribute too much to the subject and too little to the object. Schopenhauer seems to regard his refutation of the will's freedom of choice as an effort to combat this popular misconception.

Yet the conclusion reached earlier, that there can be no freedom in human action and that all human action is subject to strict necessity, is by no means Schopenhauer's last word on the matter. Only now that determinism has been completely established for all human action is it

---

[13] See *An Essay Concerning Human Understanding*, 2 vols., ed. Peter H. Nidditch (New York: Oxford University Press, 1979).

possible to seek a higher kind of freedom of the will or "true moral freedom."

Schopenhauer's continued search for human freedom is based on a fact of consciousness that has so far been left out of consideration. The fact now invoked is the clear and certain feeling of responsibility that we each have for our actions. Even the realization that our actions are inevitably necessary, given the particular constellation of the individual character and the motives involved, does not defeat our sense of responsibility. Moreover, we do not blame our actions on the motives, which are merely the varying external circumstances that occasion our actions. Instead our practice of praise and blame is directed toward the human being acting on the motives, even if that person is acting in a completely determined manner. The precise object of praise and blame, and more generally of responsibility, is the person's character, owing to which the given motives result in the given action.

In taking responsibility for an action, we are not really taking responsibility for the action as an action. We assume responsibility for that which makes our action *our* action. And that is not the motive, which is the cognition of things outside us, but the character, which is our very own inner being. Responsibility involves the satisfaction or the regret, as the case may be, over the fact that one is who one is, that one has the character that one has, as revealed in the things one did, provided certain motives. Implicit in the feeling of responsibility is, so Schopenhauer argues, the recognition that one would have acted differently had one been a different individual – a being with a different character.

Moving the discussion from the level of action to that of being or character underlying the action allows Schopenhauer to introduce an alternative conception of freedom, one that does not pertain to actions, which remain necessary, but to character, which emerges as the ultimate refuge of freedom. The freedom in question is not freedom with respect to acting but freedom in regard to being. To be sure, the freedom involved in the freedom of one's character cannot be the freedom of choice, or the ability of the will to decide one way or the other without motivational determination. The notion of the will's freedom as some choice in a situation of indifference has already been rejected as incompatible with universal natural causation.

But what could it mean to attribute freedom to one's character while maintaining the necessity of the actions following from the character? Schopenhauer argues that the freedom in question can only be understood as the freedom from the principle of sufficient reason in all of its forms, including the law of causality. Like any of the other forces of nature, the will and its basic nature or character underlies causation but is not itself a link in the causal chain. In particular, the character underlies the causal efficacy of motives but is neither motivated nor motivating. It is involved in motivational causation but not included under motivational causation.

Considered that way, the human will in general and its character in particular is no more and no less a nonphysical, a metaphysical, entity than any natural force. It could be argued that any force, not just the human will, is free as to its being while remaining completely determined in its acting. However, the wider, outright cosmological, scope of the new conception of freedom is not an issue in the topically limited *Prize Essay*. The relation of all physical reality to some metaphysical core independent of causation figures prominently, though, in Schopenhauer's writings on the philosophy of nature.[14]

But can anything more be said about the will's ultimate or original freedom from causality? To say that we are responsible for our character seems to suggest that we owe our character to ourselves, that each one of us is responsible for our own character. This seems to imply some causal process of self-constitution on the part of each and every one of us. But Schopenhauer has ruled out the applicability of any thinking in accordance with the principle of sufficient reason as inadequate to the will's radical freedom from that principle. Moreover, such a process would have to take place prior to our full-blown existence. And would this not be a reinstatement, at some more remote level, of the very freedom of choice previously rejected?

Schopenhauer attempts to clarify the nature of "true" freedom by resorting to Kant's earlier distinction between the empirical and the intelligible character of an action, which in turn builds on Kant's distinction of appearances from things in themselves in the *Critique of Pure Reason*.[15] Kant argues for the dual nature of objects. In addition to

---

[14] See *The World as Will and Representation*, vol. I, 93ff., and vol. II, 191ff.; *On the Will in Nature*, trans. Eric F. J. Payne, ed. David E. Cartwright (New York and Oxford: Berg, 1992); *On Vision and Colors*, trans. Eric F. J. Payne, ed. David E. Cartwright (Oxford and Providence, RI: Berg, 1994).

[15] A 26ff./B 42ff. and A 490ff./B 518ff.

the properties which objects exhibit under conditions of human experience, there are also those properties to be considered which objects possess, or might possess, independent of experience. The distinction is between the way things appear (to human beings) and the way they are in and of themselves. Resorting to scholastic terminology, Kant calls the empirical side or aspect or nature of things "sensible," to indicate that about the object which can be grasped by the senses. By contrast, the nonempirical side or aspect or nature of things is called "intelligible," indicating that about the object which cannot be met in experience but can only be entertained in thought by the intellect.

Kant applies the distinction throughout nature and pays special attention to its import for actions of all kinds and human actions in particular. In Kant's usage, "character" designates quite generally the law governing the efficacy of a cause.[16] The empirical character of a cause, and by extension of an agent, is the empirical law that links appearances in natural-causal terms. In addition, Kant countenances the intelligible character of a cause or agent, which pertains to the latter's intelligible side, aspect, or nature. Hence Kant allows for a dual causality or two types of causality with respect to one and the same action or, more generally speaking, one and the same event. A given action or event can have both an empirical and a nonempirical cause, the former due to its empirical character, the latter due to its intelligible character.[17]

In the *Critique of Pure Reason*, Kant treats the dualism of empirical and intelligible character as a mere logical possibility, something that cannot be excluded on logical grounds alone and for which positive evidence might be discovered in later investigations, specifically in the theory of morals. Kant's specific point in introducing the distinction is to argue that necessity and freedom need not contradict each other in the description of an action. An action may well be correctly described as naturally caused, while admitting, or perhaps requiring, a further description under which the event is brought about by something other than natural causes operating under natural causal laws. To the extent that the action is brought about by something other than natural causes, it can be described as free. Kant's full conception of nonnatural

---

[16] See *Critique of Pure Reason*, A 539/B 567.
[17] See *Critique of Pure Reason*, A 532ff./B 560ff.

causation includes the introduction of a nonnatural law for the naturally free action, viz., the moral law.[18]

Schopenhauer draws on Kant's distinction between empirical and intelligible character to show how freedom and necessity need not contradict each other when attributed to one and the same action. The freedom so reconciled with natural necessity is the freedom from natural necessity. It is important to note that in his selective appropriation Schopenhauer does not follow Kant's identification of freedom as an alternative type of causality, subject to its own, nonnatural law (moral law). For Schopenhauer, any application of the principle of sufficient reason, including its causal form, fails to capture the true nature of freedom.

The exclusion of freedom from the domain of rational inquiry under the guidance of the principle of sufficient reason seems to render impossible any further thought about such freedom and the will to which it might pertain. At this point, Schopenhauer's specific examination of freedom converges with his more general metaphysics according to which the world considered in itself is best described as *will* – on the analogy with the human will known to us through inner as well as outer experience. The will in the extended, cosmological sense is supposed to be the essence of the world as it exists outside and independent of the relations of ground and consequence that obtain within the world as experienced, or – in Schopenhauer's phrase – the world as representation.

Schopenhauer rejects the idea that the will, either in its limited psychological or in its universal cosmological function, can be described in causal or quasi-causal terms. Instead he wants us to think of the will as the hidden other side, the inner side or inside of the overt world of experience. The suggestion is that the essence of the world, including the solution to the problem of the will's freedom, lies not behind this world in some other world but within this our world. With respect to the will's freedom, Schopenhauer brings out this faithfulness to our world in the statement that "freedom is transcendental." His use of the Kantian term indicates not a leaving behind of experience but a turn

---

[18] See *Groundwork of the Metaphysics of Morals*, trans. Mary Gregor, in Immanuel Kant, *Practical Philosophy*, trans. and ed. Mary Gregor (Cambridge: Cambridge University Press, 1996), 440. The *Groundwork of the Metaphysics of Morals* is cited after the pagination of the work in vol. IV of the Academy edition indicated in the standard modern editions and translations of the work. See also *Critique of Practical Reason*, Academy edition, V, 30.

toward its very core, which for Schopenhauer, though, can no longer be described in the Kantian language of "conditions" and "grounds."

It is important to keep in mind this transcendental (as opposed to transcending) character of freedom, its immanent transcendence, when considering Schopenhauer's concluding reference to a pronouncement he attributes to the seventeenth-century French philosopher, Catholic theologian, and priest Nicholas Malebranche and which also serves as the motto of the *Prize Essay*: "La liberté est un mystère" (freedom is a mystery). The exact quotation is nowhere to be found in Malebranche's works.[19] However, the phrase "is a mystery" occurs in Malebranche's discussion of the relation between mind and body.[20] In another context the compatibility of freedom and divine foreknowledge regarding human action is called "a mystery."[21] In the first case, the mystery concerns God's will to have human beings be embodied rather than be pure spirits. In the second case, the mystery concerns the relation of human freedom to divine omniscience. Schopenhauer's claim about the mysterious freedom of the human will is different from either of those cases. There is no appeal to unknown and perhaps unknowable divine reasons for human freedom. Nor is there the threat to human freedom posed by divine powers. The mystery about the will's freedom does not lie outside the world but resides in the world itself. To be sure, freedom is not to be found in the world as representation or the world known under the forms of space, time, and causality. In that case freedom would be the miraculous suspension of the natural order. Instead freedom belongs to the world as will – to its core as revealed in our emotional life, which includes the feeling of responsibility. To Schopenhauer, freedom is a mystery but not a miracle.

---

[19] Arthur Hübscher has traced the wording of the motto of the *Prize Essay* to a work by the eighteenth-century French philosopher Claude-Adrien Helvétius (*De l'esprit* [On the mind], 1758), with which Schopenhauer was familiar. See "*La liberté est un mystère*. Das Motto der norwegischen Preisschrift," *Schopenhauer-Jahrbuch* 45 (1964): 26–30.

[20] *Dialogues on Metaphysics and Religion*, ed. and trans. Nicholas Jolley and David Scott (Cambridge: Cambridge University Press, 1997), 63.

[21] *The Search After Truth*, ed. and trans. Thomas M. Lennon and Paul J. Olscamp (Cambridge: Cambridge University Press, 1997), vol. III, 1.

Chronology

1788	Born 22 February in the free city of Danzig (today's Gdansk, Poland), the first and only son of the Hanseatic merchant Heinrich Floris Schopenhauer and his wife Johanna, née Trosiener
1793	In response to the imminent annexation of Danzig by Prussia, Heinrich Floris Schopenhauer moves his family and the firm to the free city of Hamburg
1797–99	Lives with the French family of one of his father's business partners in Le Havre
1799–1803	Attends a private school in Hamburg
1803–4	Accompanies his parents on a tour of Europe (Holland, England, France, Switzerland, Austria) as reward for agreeing to pursue a career as a merchant rather than as a scholar
1804–7	Apprenticed to two Hanseatic merchants in Hamburg
1805	20 April: death of Heinrich Floris Schopenhauer, probably by suicide
1806	Johanna Schopenhauer along with her daughter Adele (b. 1797) moves to Weimar, where she establishes herself as a literary hostess and popular novelist
1807–9	Leaves his merchant apprenticeship and prepares for university studies, first at the Gymnasium in Gotha and then through private tutoring in Weimar
1809–11	Studies sciences and philosophy at the University of Göttingen

1811–13	Studies sciences and philosophy at the University of Berlin, where he attends the lectures of Fichte and Schleiermacher
1813	Lives in Rudolstadt near Weimar and writes his doctoral dissertation, *On the Fourfold Root of the Principle of Sufficient Reason*, which is accepted by the University of Jena and published in 1814
1813–14	Lives in his mother's house in Weimar. Has contacts with Goethe, with whom he discusses the theory of colors. In May 1814 the longstanding conflicts with his mother culminate in the final break
1814–18	Lives in Dresden
1815	Publishes *On Vision and Colors*
1818	March: completes his main work, *The World as Will and Representation*, which is published in January 1819
1818–19	Travels in Italy (Florence, Rome, Naples, Venice). Returns to Dresden
1819–31	Privatdozent (unsalaried lecturer) at the University of Berlin. The only lecture course he actually gives takes place in the summer semester of 1820
1822–23	Travels in Italy (Milan, Florence, Venice)
1823–25	Lives in Bad Gastein (Switzerland), Mannheim, and Dresden
1825–31	Lives in Berlin
1831–32	Lives in Frankfurt-on-Main
1832–33	Lives in Mannheim
1833–60	Lives in Frankfurt-on-Main
1835	Publishes *On the Will in Nature*
1839	Awarded prize for essay *On the Freedom of the Will*, which is published in 1841 together with his unsuccessful prize essay *On the Basis of Morality*, under the title *The Two Basic Problems of Ethics*
1844	Publishes second edition of *The World as Will and Representation*, which contains a second, supplementary volume
1851	Publishes *Parerga and Paralipomena*
1853	An anonymous article on Schopenhauer, entitled

"Iconoclasm in German Philosophy," appears in *Westminster and Foreign Quarterly Review*, marking the beginning of his public recognition

1860   Dies on 21 September in Frankfurt-on-Main

Further reading

Two detailed intellectual biographies of Schopenhauer are available in English translation, the first by Schopenhauer's main German editor in the twentieth century, the second by a master raconteur: Arthur Hübscher, *The Philosophy of Schopenhauer in its Intellectual Context*, trans. Joachim T. Baer and David E. Cartwright (Lewiston, NY: Edwin Mellen Press, 1989), and Rüdiger Safranski, *Schopenhauer and the Wild Years of Philosophy*, trans. Ewald Osers (Cambridge, MA: Harvard University Press, 1990). Bryan Magee, *The Philosophy of Schopenhauer* (Oxford: Clarendon Press, 1983; revised and enlarged edition 1997), combines a succinct account of Schopenhauer's philosophy with detailed studies of his relation to earlier and later philosophical, religious, literary, and artistic figures and movements, including Ludwig Wittgenstein and Richard Wagner.

A comprehensive treatment of Schopenhauer's metaphysics is John E. Atwell, *Schopenhauer on the Character of the World: The Metaphysics of Will* (Berkeley, Los Angeles, and London: University of California Press, 1995). The entire first part of Atwell's earlier work, *Schopenhauer: The Human Character* (Philadelphia: Temple University Press, 1990), is devoted to Schopenhauer's theory of human action. Chapters or sections on Schopenhauer's ethics and his theory of the human will are to be found in the following studies: Patrick Gardiner, *Schopenhauer* (Baltimore: Penguin, 1963), D. W. Hamlyn, *Schopenhauer* (London: Routledge & Kegan Paul, 1980), Julian Young, *Willing and Unwilling: A Study in the Philosophy of Schopenhauer* (Dordrecht and Boston: Martinus Nijhoff, 1987), and Christopher Janaway, *Self and World in Schopenhauer's Philosophy* (Oxford: Clarendon Press, 1988). Main aspects and problems of Schopenhauer's philosophy are discussed in three recent collections of articles: Michael Fox, ed., *Schopenhauer: His Philosophical Achievement* (Totowa, NJ: Barnes & Noble, 1980), Eric van der Luft, ed., *Schopenhauer: New Essays on His 200th Birthday* (Lewiston, NY: Edwin Mellen Press, 1988), and Christopher Janaway, ed., *The Cambridge Companion to Schopenhauer* (Cambridge: Cambridge University Press, forthcoming).

Further readings in Schopenhauer best begin with the study of his doctoral dissertation, *On the Fourfold Root of the Principle of Sufficient Reason*, trans. Eric F. J. Payne (La Salle, IL: Open Court, 1974), as recommended by Schopenhauer himself, and from there should proceed to *The World as Will and Representation*, 2 vols., trans. Eric F. J. Payne (New York: Dover, 1966), the first volume of which contains Schopenhauer's epistemology (Book One), metaphysics of nature (Book Two), aesthetics (Book Three), and ethics (Book Four), supplemented by correlated chapters in the second volume as well as by Schopenhauer's discussion of "corroborations from the empirical sciences" of his philosophy in *On the Will in Nature*, trans. Eric F. J. Payne, ed. with an introduction by David E. Cartwright (New York and Oxford: Berg, 1992). Further readings in Schopenhauer's ethics might include the other (unsuccessful) prize essay, *On the Basis of Morality*, trans. Eric F. J. Payne (Indianapolis: Bobbs-Merrill, 1965; revised edition with an introduction by David E. Cartwright, Providence, RI and Oxford: Berghahn, 1995), and several of the shorter philosophical essays gathered by Schopenhauer himself under the title *Parerga and Paralipomena*, 2 vols., trans. Eric F. J. Payne (New York: Dover, 1966).

Note on the text and translation

Source of the translation

This translation of Schopenhauer's *Prize Essay on the Freedom of the Will* was found among the papers of the late Eric Payne, who translated all of Schopenhauer's published works and most of his unpublished writings into English but never saw the present translation through to publication. The translation is based on the second edition of the *Prize Essay* published in 1860. In preparing this edition I checked Payne's typescript, which probably dates from the late 1950s, against the critical edition of the *Prize Essay* in vol. IV of Arthur Schopenhauer, *Sämtliche Werke*, ed. A. Hübscher, 3rd ed. (Wiesbaden: F. A. Brockhaus, 1972). As in his translations of Schopenhauer's other published works, Payne relied on this superbly annotated edition, which first appeared in 1937–41, for the identification of quotations and references in the *Prize Essay*.

Although Payne's translation of the *Prize Essay* is complete, it is quite possible – even likely – that he would have refined his work even further in preparation for actual publication. Under the circumstances, I have done so on his behalf and made a fair number of changes in the interest of accuracy and readability, always following the principle of departing from Payne's typescript only when needed. I have added several explanatory editorial footnotes to Payne's translator's footnotes. Schopenhauer's own notes are identified by letter.

The *Prize Essay on the Freedom of the Will* first appeared in Norwegian translation in 1840 published by the Royal Norwegian Society of Sciences, which had awarded its prize to the work. In 1841

Schopenhauer published the German original, along with a second prize essay, *On the Basis of Morality* (*Über die Grundlage der Moral*) (to which the Royal Danish Society of Sciences had not awarded a prize in another competition), and an introduction attacking the Danish Academy for its negative judgment, all under the title *The Two Basic Problems of Ethics* (*Die beiden Grundprobleme der Ethik*). Schopenhauer was able to prepare the second edition of the latter work, adding a new preface that again berates the Danish Academy, but he had already died when the volume came out in 1860. Payne's translation of *On the Basis of Morality*, which includes the prefaces to the first and second editions of *The Two Basic Problems of Ethics*, first appeared in 1965; a revised edition was published in 1995.

Features of the translation

It is a hallmark of Payne's translations of Schopenhauer that they preserve as much as possible the stylistic qualities and literary appearance of the German original. This is also true of his translation of the *Prize Essay*. In particular, Payne retains to a large extent Schopenhauer's often long, but always clearly structured, sentences. The same holds for Schopenhauer's allocation of emphasis to proper names and quotations from foreign languages, and his use of dashes to set off different sections within a paragraph and to mark omissions in quotations.

Payne also follows Schopenhauer's customary practice of citing and quoting Greek, Latin, French, Italian, and English sources in the original languages in the main body of the text, with the Greek quotations followed by Latin translations. The only German translations that Schopenhauer provides are of the English quotations. In Payne's translation the German renditions of English quotations have been dropped, and English translations of all quotations in foreign languages have been provided in notes by the translator. Payne's translations of Schopenhauer's quotations in foreign languages are based on the German translations provided in *Sämtliche Werke*, vol. VII, 287–91.

The original titles of the works quoted or cited by Schopenhauer have been preserved in the main body of the text, with English translations provided in notes by the editor. An exception to this are Aristotle's and Kant's works, which are referred to by their standard English titles throughout the translated text.

By retaining Schopenhauer's inclusion of foreign-language material in the main body of the text and relegating the translations to the notes, Payne's translation manages to recreate for the English-speaking reader what it is like to read Schopenhauer in the original – which is not always German – while providing the linguistic help required by most readers today.

The marginal numbers refer to the pagination of the edition of the *Prize Essay* in vol. IV of *Sämtliche Werke*.

Bibliographical references

Virtually all of Schopenhauer's references to other works, including some of his own, can be traced readily to modern editions where these are available. "Lib." refers to the book (*liber*), "c." to the chapter (*caput*) and "§" to the section or paragraph of a given text. In the references to Aristotle I have supplemented Schopenhauer's references with the standard pagination (Bekker). In the case of Schelling's *Philosophical Inquiries into the Nature of Human Freedom*, which Schopenhauer cites from an old German edition, I have supplied references to a current English translation. For Kant's *Prolegomena to Any Future Metaphysics* and *Critique of Practical Reason*, which Schopenhauer cites after the first editions, I have provided notes with references to the pagination of volumes IV and V of the Academy edition of Kant's collected works (*Kant's gesammelte Schriften*, ed. Royal Prussian Academy of Sciences [Berlin: Reimer, 1903 and 1908]). The pagination of the Academy edition is included in the recent English translations of these works. Kant's *Critique of Pure Reason* is cited by Schopenhauer after the first and fifth editions, of which the paginations coincide with those of the first and second editions of the work ("A" and "B", respectively) provided in the translations of the *Critique* by Norman Kemp Smith (New York: St. Martin's, 1965), Werner Pluhar (Indianapolis: Hackett, 1996), and Paul Guyer and Allen Wood (Cambridge: Cambridge University Press, 1998). The A and B pagination is also employed in the additional textual references to the *Critique* which I have provided in several notes.

English translations of the works by Schopenhauer to which he himself refers are listed above in "Further Reading."

Terminology

In editing Payne's translation, I have paid special attention to making Schopenhauer's terminology consistent with that employed in recent translations of Kant's works, on which Schopenhauer's terms and concepts are based. In particular, I have departed from Payne's rendition of *Anschauung* as "perception," to be found in his published translations of Schopenhauer, and replaced it with the Kantian "intuition" and its derivatives "intuited" (for *angeschaut*) and "intuitive" (for *anschaulich*), thus reserving "perception" for the translation of *Wahrnehmung*. Moreover, I have rendered most occurrences of *Erkenntnis* and *Kenntnis* and all occurrences of their plural forms (*Erkenntnisse* and *Kenntnisse*) with "cognition" and "cognitions," respectively, departing from Payne's uniform use of "knowledge." Accordingly, *Erkenntnisvermögen* is translated as "faculty of cognition" and *Erkenntniskraft* as "cognitive power." The English word "cognition" is more suited to rendering the procedural and fallible character of *Erkenntnis*, as opposed to the epistemic certainty and truth typically expressed by *Wissen*. Therefore I have restricted the use of "knowledge" for *Erkenntnis* or *Kenntnis* to those cases in which the terms designate the certainty or truth of the result of some cognitive process.

Willkürlich is rendered as "voluntary" (changed form Payne's "arbitrary"). The Latin phrase *liberum arbitrium*, frequently employed by Schopenhauer, is translated as "free choice of the will" (changed from Payne's "the will's free decision"). Finally, Schopenhauer's derogatory term *Rockenphilosophie*, which occurs several times in his writings, refers not to a female undergarment, as suggested by Payne's translation "petticoat philosophy," but to the distaff (*Rocken*) employed in spinning. Schopenhauer likens the philosophy so designated to the verbal byproduct of this domestic activity. I have chosen the phrase "spinning-wheel philosophy" instead.

The German *Grund* is rendered as "ground," except in the phrase *zureichender Grund*, as in *Satz vom zureichenden Grund* (principle of sufficient reason), where it is rendered as "reason." *Inbegriff*, in contradistinction to *Begriff* (concept), is translated as "conceptual complex." *Sein* is translated as "being," *Wesen* as "essence," and *Existenz* as "existence." *Gnadenwahl* is rendered as "predestination." The scholastic term *Affection* (plural *Affectionen*), as in *Affectionen des Willens*, meaning determination or mode, is translated as "affection" or "affections" (as in "affections of the will") and to is be distinguished from *Affect* (plural *Affecte*), meaning sudden emotional reaction, rendered as "affect" or "affects."

Prize Essay on the Freedom of the Will

awarded the prize by the
Royal Norwegian Society of
Sciences
at Trontheim on 26 January 1839

La liberté est un mystère.
(Freedom is a mystery.)

3   The question set by the Royal Society is as follows:

> *Num liberum hominum arbitrium e sui ipsius conscientia demonstrari potest?*

"Can the freedom of the human will be demonstrated from self-consciousness?"

I
Definitions

With so important, serious, and difficult a question that is essentially identical with one of the main problems of all medieval and modern philosophy, great accuracy and hence an analysis of the principal concepts coming within its purview are certainly not out of place.

(1) *What is meant by freedom?*

Carefully considered, this concept is *negative*. By it we understand simply the absence of everything that impedes and obstructs; however, the latter as something manifesting force must be something positive. In keeping with the possible nature of this impeding something, the concept has three very different subspecies, namely physical, intellectual, and moral freedom.

(a) *Physical freedom* is the absence of *material* obstacles of every kind. Thus we speak of free sky, free view, free air, free field, a free place, free
4   heat (that is not chemically bound), free electricality, free course of a stream where it is no longer checked by mountains or sluices, and so on.[1] Even free room, free board, free press, postage-free indicate the absence of onerous conditions that, as hindrances to pleasure, usually attach to such things. But in our thinking, the concept of freedom is most frequently predicated of animals. The characteristic of animals is that their movements proceed from *their will*, are voluntary, and consequently are called *free* when no material obstacle makes this impossible. Now since these obstacles may be of very different kinds, but that which they obstruct is always *the will*, it is preferable, for the sake of simplicity, to take the concept from the positive side, and with it

---

[1] The extensive use of "free" to designate the lack of a physical obstacle is more idiomatic in German than in English.

to think of everything that moves only by its will or acts only from its will. This transformation of the concept essentially alters nothing. Accordingly, in this *physical* meaning of the concept of freedom, animals and human beings are called *free* when neither chains, dungeon, nor paralysis, and thus generally no *physical, material* obstacle impedes their actions, but these occur in accordance with their *will*.

This *physical meaning* of the concept of freedom, and especially as the predicate of animals, is the original, immediate, and therefore most frequent one. For this reason, the concept given this meaning is not subject to any doubt or controversy, but its reality can always be verified by experience. For as soon as an animal acts only from its *will*, it is in this sense *free*; and no account is taken here of what may have influenced its will itself. For in this, its original, immediate, and therefore popular meaning, the concept of freedom refers only to an *ability*, that is, precisely to the absence of *physical* obstacles to the actions of the animal. Thus we say that the birds of the air, the animals of the forest are free; human beings are free by nature; only the free are happy. A people is also called free, and by this we understand that it is governed only by laws and that it itself has issued them; for then in every case it obeys only its own will. Accordingly, political freedom is to be classed under physical freedom.

5   But as soon as we leave this *physical* freedom and consider the other two kinds, we are concerned no longer with the popular, but with the *philosophical* sense of the concept, which, as is well known, opens the way to many difficulties. It is divisible into two entirely different kinds, namely intellectual and moral freedom.

(b) *Intellectual freedom*, τὸ ἑκούσιον καὶ ἀκούσιον κατὰ διάνοιαν[2] in Aristotle,[3] is taken into consideration here merely for the purpose of making the classification complete. I therefore propose to defer its discussion until the very end of this essay, for by then the concepts to be used therein will have found their explanation already in what has gone before, so that it can be dealt with briefly then. But in the classification it had to come next to physical freedom, since it is most closely related to the latter.

(c) I therefore turn at once to the third kind, to *moral freedom*, which

---

[2] "The voluntary and involuntary with respect to thought."
[3] Aristotle (384–322 B.C.): Greek philosopher; the phrase cited by Schopenhauer can be found in *Eudemian Ethics*, II, 7, 1223a 23–25 and elsewhere.

is really the *liberum arbitrium*[4] mentioned in the question of the Royal Society.

This concept is connected with that of physical freedom in a manner that also enables us to see its necessarily much later origin. As I have said, physical freedom refers only to material obstacles, and exists at once with the absence of the latter. But in a good many cases it was observed that, without being impeded by material obstacles, a human being was restrained from acting as otherwise would certainly have been in accordance with his will, by mere motives, such as threats, promises, dangers, and the like. The question was therefore raised whether such a human being had still been *free*, or whether, like a physical obstacle, a strong countermotive could actually prevent and render impossible an action according to the will proper. The answer to this could not be difficult for sound common sense, namely that a motive could never act like a physical obstacle, since the latter might easily exceed absolutely the physical forces of a human being, whereas a motive can never be irresistible in itself or have absolute power but may

6   still always be overcome by a *stronger countermotive*, if only it were present and the human being in the given individual case could be determined by it. For we frequently see that even what is usually the strongest of all motives, the preservation of life, is nevertheless overcome by others, e.g., in suicide and the sacrifice of life for others, for opinions and for interests of many kinds; and conversely, that occasionally all degrees of the most extreme tortures on the rack have been surmounted by the mere thought that life would otherwise be lost. But although it was evident from this that motives have no purely objective and absolute compulsion, a subjective and relative one could nevertheless belong to them, namely for the person concerned; and in the end this was the same thing. Hence there remains the question: Is the will itself free? – Here then the concept of freedom, which one had hitherto thought of only in reference to the *ability to act*, was now brought in relation to *willing*, and the problem arose whether willing itself was *free*. But on further consideration, the original, purely empirical, and hence popular concept of freedom proved incapable of entering into this connection with *willing*. For according to this concept, "*free*" means "*in conformity with one's own will*." Now if we

---

[4] "Free choice of the will."

ask whether the will itself is free, we are asking whether it is in conformity with itself; and this of course is self-evident, but it also tells us nothing. As a result of the empirical concept of freedom we have: "I am free, if I can *do what I will*," and the freedom is already decided by this "what I will." But now since we are asking about the freedom of *willing* itself, this question should accordingly be expressed as follows: "Can you also *will* what you will?" This appears as if the willing depended on yet another willing lying behind it. And supposing that this question were answered in the affirmative, there would soon arise the second question: "Can you also will what you will to will?" and thus it would be pushed back to infinity, since we would always think of *one* willing as being dependent on a previous or deeper willing, and thus in vain endeavor to arrive ultimately at a willing that we were bound to conceive and accept as being dependent on absolutely nothing. However, if we wanted to assume such a willing, we could just as well assume the first as any final willing that had been arbitrarily chosen. Yet in this way the question would be reduced to the quite simple one of "can you will?" But whether the mere answering of it in the affirmative decides the freedom of willing is what we wanted to know, and is left unsettled. The original, empirical concept of freedom, a concept drawn from doing, thus refuses to enter into a direct connection with that of willing. Therefore to be able to apply to the will the concept of freedom, one had to modify it by grasping it in a more abstract way. This was done by conceiving through the concept of *freedom* only the absence of all *necessity* in general. Here the concept retains the *negative* character which I had assigned to it at the very beginning. Accordingly, the concept of *necessity*, as the positive concept establishing the former's negative meaning, would have to be discussed first.

We therefore ask what is meant by *necessary*. The usual explanation, that "necessary is that the opposite of which is impossible, or which cannot be otherwise," is merely verbal, a paraphrase of the concept which does not increase our insight. But as the real definition I give the following: *necessary is that which follows from a given sufficient ground.* Like every correct definition, this proposition is capable also of inversion. Now depending on whether this sufficient ground is logical, mathematical, or physical (i.e., causal), the *necessity* will be logical (like that of the conclusion when the premises are given), mathematical (e.g., the equality of the sides of the triangle if the angles are equal), or physical and real (like the occurrence of the effect as soon as the cause exists). In each case, the necessity adheres to the consequent with equal strictness if the ground is given. Only insofar as we understand something as the consequent of a given ground do we recognize it as necessary; and conversely, as soon as we recognize something as a consequent of a sufficient ground, we see that it is necessary; for all grounds are compelling. This real definition is so adequate and exhaustive that necessity and being the consequence of a given sufficient ground are outright convertible terms, in other words, the one can always be put in the place of the other.[a] – Accordingly, absence of necessity would be identical with absence of a determining sufficient ground. Now the contingent is conceived as the opposite of the *necessary*; but the one does not contradict the other. For everything contingent is only *relatively* so. For in the real world, where only the contingent is to be found, every event is *necessary* in regard to its cause; but in regard to everything else with which it coincides in time and space, it is *contingent*. Now as absence of necessity is characteristic of what is free, the latter would have to be dependent on absolutely no cause at all, and consequently would have to be defined as the *absolutely contingent*. This is an extremely problematical concept, one whose conceivability I cannot vouch for, and one which nevertheless coincides in a curious way with the concept of *freedom*. In any case, the *free* remains that which is in no relation necessary; and this means that which is dependent on no ground. Now this concept, applied to the will of a human being, would state that in its manifestations (acts of will) an individual will would not be determined by causes or sufficient reasons in general, for otherwise its acts would not be free but necessary, since the consequent of a given ground (whatever the nature of that ground) is always *necessary*. On this rest *Kant's* definition according to which freedom is the power to initiate *of itself* a series of changes.[5] For this "of itself," when reduced to its true meaning, signifies "without antecedent cause"; this, however, is identical with "without necessity." Thus, although that definition gives the concept of freedom the appearance of being positive, on closer examination its

[5] See Immanuel Kant, *Critique of Pure Reason*, A 445/B 473.

[a] A discussion of the concept of necessity will be found in my treatise *On the Fourfold Root of the Principle of Sufficient Reason*, second edition, § 49.

negative nature is again apparent. – A free will would therefore be one that was not determined by grounds; and since everything determining something else must be a ground – a real ground, i.e., a cause, in the case of real things – a free will would be one that was determined by nothing at all. The particular manifestations of such a will (acts of will) would therefore proceed absolutely and quite originally from itself, without being brought about necessarily by antecedent conditions, and thus without being determined by anything according to a rule. In the case of such a concept clear thinking is at an end because the principle of sufficient reason in all its meanings is the essential form of our whole faculty of cognition, yet here it is supposed to be given up. However, we are not left without even a *terminus technicus* for this concept; it is *liberum arbitrium indifferentiae*.[6] Moreover, this is the only clearly determined, firm, and settled concept of that which is called freedom of the will. Therefore one cannot depart from it without falling into vague and hazy explanations behind which lurks a hesitant insufficiency, as when one speaks of grounds that do not necessarily bring about their consequents. Every consequence of a ground is necessary, and every necessity is a consequence of a ground. From the assumption of such a *liberum arbitrium indifferentiae*, the immediate consequence that characterizes this concept itself and is therefore to be stated as its mark is that for a human individual endowed with it, under given external circumstances that are determined quite individually and thoroughly, two diametrically opposed actions are equally possible.

(2) *What is meant by self-consciousness?*

Answer: The consciousness of *our own self* in contrast to the consciousness of *other things*; the latter is the faculty of cognition. Now before those other things ever occur in it, the faculty of cognition contains certain forms of the mode and manner of that occurrence, and accordingly such forms are conditions of the possibility of their objective existence, that is, of their existence as objects for us; as is well known, these forms are time, space, and causality. Now although those forms of cognition reside within us, this is only for our becoming conscious *of other things* as such and always with reference to the latter.

---

[6] "Free choice of indifference."

And so, although those forms reside within us, we must not regard them as belonging to *self-consciousness*, but rather as rendering possible *the consciousness of other things*, i.e., objective cognition.

10   Further I shall not be tempted by the ambiguity of the word *conscientia*,[7] used in the question, into including in self-consciousness those moral impulses of human beings known under the name of conscience, or practical reason with its categorical imperatives as maintained by Kant. I shall not be led astray because such impulses occur only as a consequence of experience and reflection and hence of the consciousness of other things; and also because the borderline has not yet been clearly and incontestably drawn between what in those impulses is original and peculiar to human nature, and what is added by moral and religious education. Moreover it can hardly be the Royal Society's intention, by drawing conscience into self-consciousness, to have the question moved over to the grounds of morality, to repeat *Kant's* moral proof or rather postulate of freedom from the moral law that is known *a priori*, on the strength of the conclusion "you can because you ought."[8]

From what has been said it is clear that by far the greatest part of all our consciousness in general is not *self-consciousness* but the *consciousness of other things* or the faculty of cognition. The latter with all its powers is directed outward, and is the scene (indeed, the condition, if we go more deeply into the matter) of the real outer world. It reacts to the latter by apprehending it first through intuition; it then ruminates, so to speak, on what has been gained in this way, and works it up into concepts. *Thinking* consists in the endless combinations of concepts which are carried out with the aid of words. – Thus *self-consciousness* would be only what we retain after subtracting this by far the largest part of our whole consciousness. From this we see already that the wealth of self-consciousness cannot be very great; and so if there should actually reside in self-consciousness the data that are sought for demonstrating the freedom of the will, we may hope they will not escape us. It has also been advanced that an *inner sense*[b] constitutes the

---

[7] Lexically speaking, the Latin term "conscientia" used in the prize question can mean both "consciousness" and "conscience." However, its occurrence in the phrase "ipsius conscientia" ("*conscientia* of oneself") rules out the latter meaning on linguistic grounds.

[8] See *Critique of Practical Reason*, Academy edition, v, 30.

[b] It is found already in Cicero (Marcus Tullius Cicero [106–43 B.C.]: Roman orator, statesman, writer, and philosopher) as *tactus interior*: *Academica* (*Academic Questions*), I, 7. More clearly in Augustine (Saint Augustine [354–430]: Christian theologian and philosopher), *De libero arbitrio*

11 organ of self-consciousness. This, however, is to be understood figuratively rather than literally, for self-consciousness is immediate. Be that as it may, our next question is what self-consciousness contains, or how a human being becomes immediately conscious of its own self. Answer: Absolutely and entirely as one who *wills*. Everyone who observes his own self-consciousness will soon become aware that its object is at all times his own willing. By this, however, we must understand not merely the definite acts of will that lead at once to deeds, and the explicit decisions together with the actions resulting from them. On the contrary, whoever is capable of grasping in any way that which is essential, in spite of the different modifications of degree and kind, will have no hesitation in reckoning as manifestations of willing all desiring, striving, wishing, longing, yearning, hoping, loving, rejoicing, exulting, and the like, as well as the feeling of unwillingness or repugnance, detesting, fleeing, fearing, being angry, hating, mourning, suffering, in short, all affects and passions. For these are only movements more or less weak or strong, stirrings at one moment violent and stormy, at another mild and faint, of our own will that is either checked or given its way, satisfied or unsatisfied. They all refer in many different ways to the attainment or missing of what is desired, and to the enduring or subduing of what is abhorred. They are therefore definite affections of the same will that is active in decisions and actions.[c] Even what are called feelings of pleasure and displeasure are included in the list above; it is true that they exist in a great variety of degrees and kinds; yet they

12 can always be reduced to affections of desire or abhorrence and thus to the will itself becoming conscious of itself as satisfied or unsatisfied, impeded or allowed its way. Indeed, this extends even to bodily

(*On the Free Choice of the Will*), II, 3ff. Then in Descartes (René Descartes [1596–1650]: French philosopher and mathematician), *Principia philosophiae* (*Principles of Philosophy*), IV, 190; and in Locke (John Locke [1632–1704]: English philosopher, statesman, and physician) it is fully described. [Schopenhauer's note, except for the parenthetical information.]

[c] It is very remarkable that the Church Father *Augustine* was perfectly aware of this, whereas so many of the moderns with their pretended "faculty of feeling" do not see it. Thus in *De civitate Dei* (*The City of God*), lib. XIV, c. 6, he speaks of the *affectiones animi* (affective states of the mind), which in the preceding book he brought under four categories, *cupiditas, timor, laetitia, tristitia* (desire, fear, joy, sadness), and he says: *voluntas est quippe in omnibus, imo omnes nihil aliud, quam voluntates sunt: nam quid est cupiditas et laetitia, nisi voluntas in eorum consensionem, quae volumus? et quid est metus atque tristitia, nisi voluntas in dissensionem ab his quae nolumus?* (In them all [desire, fear, joy, sadness] the will is to be found; in fact they are all nothing but affections of the will. For what are desire and joy but the will to consent to what we want? And what are fear and sadness but the will not to consent to what we do not want?) [Schopenhauer's note, except for the parenthetical information.]

sensations, pleasant or painful, and to all the countless sensations lying between these two extremes. For the essence of all these affections consists in their entering immediately into self-consciousness as something agreeable or disagreeable to the will. If we carefully consider the matter, we are immediately conscious of our own body only as the outwardly acting organ of the will, and as the seat of receptivity for pleasant or painful sensations. But, as I have just said, these sensations themselves go back to immediate affections of the will which are either agreeable or disagreeable to it. Whether or not we include these mere feelings of pleasure or displeasure, we shall in any case find that all those movements of the will, those variations of willing and not-willing, which with their constant ebb and flow constitute the only object of self-consciousness, or, if the term be preferred, of inner sense, stand in a thoroughgoing and universally acknowledged relation to what is perceived and known in the external world. However, the latter, as already stated, lies no longer in the province of immediate *self-consciousness*, whose limits are reached by us where it passes into the domain of the *consciousness of other things* as soon as we come into contact with the external world. But the objects perceived in the latter are the material and occasion for all those movements and acts of the will. We shall not take this to be a *petitio principii*;[9] for no one can deny that our willing is concerned always with external objects, is directed to them, revolves around them, and is at any rate occasioned by them in their capacity as motives. For otherwise one would be left with a will completely cut off from the external world and imprisoned in the dark inside of self-consciousness. What is for us still problematical is merely the necessity with which those objects that are situated in the external world determine the acts of the will.

13   We therefore find that self-consciousness is very greatly, properly speaking even exclusively, concerned with the *will*. But whether such self-consciousness in this its sole material finds the data from which the *freedom* of that very will would result in the previously discussed and only clear and definite sense of the word is the aim we have in view. We will now steer straight for it after all this tacking, in the course of which we have already come appreciably nearer to it.

---

[9] "Begging of the question."

II
The will before self-consciousness

When a human being *wills*, he wills something; his act of will is always directed to an object and is conceivable only in reference to such. Now what is meant by willing something? This means that the act of will, which is itself in the first instance only an object of self-consciousness, arises on the occasion of something that belongs to the consciousness of *other things* and thus is an object of the faculty of cognition. In this connection such an object is called a *motive* and is at the same time the material of the act of will, in that the latter is directed to it, that is to say, aims at some change in it, and thus reacts to it; its whole essence consists in this *reaction*. It is clear from this that without the motive the act of will could not occur, for it would lack the occasion as well as the material. But the question is whether, if this object exists for the faculty of cognition, the act of will *must* now occur, or rather could fail to occur, and either no act of will may arise, or one that is quite different or even an opposite one; hence whether that reaction may also fail to appear, or, under entirely the same circumstances, prove to be different or even the very opposite. Briefly, the question is whether the act of will is necessarily called forth by the motive, or whether the will retains complete freedom to will or not to will, when the motive enters consciousness. Here, then, we have the concept of freedom in the abstract sense previously discussed and shown to be the only one applicable here, as the mere negation of necessity, and consequently our problem is posed. But we have to seek the data for its solution in immediate *self-consciousness*, and to this end we shall thoroughly examine the statement of self-consciousness, and not cut the knot by a summary decision, as *Descartes* did when he simply stated: *Libertatis*

14

15

autem et indifferentiae, quae in nobis est, nos ita conscios esse, ut nihil sit, quod evidentius et perfectius comprendamus (*Principia philosophiae*, I, § 41).[1] The inadmissibility of this assertion has already been censured by *Leibniz* (*Théodicée*, I, § 50 and III, § 292);[2] yet on this point he himself was only a reed swaying in the wind. After the most contradictory statements, he finally arrived at the result that the will is certainly inclined, but not necessitated by motives. Thus he says: *Omnes actiones sunt determinatae, et nunquam indifferentes, quia semper datur ratio inclinans quidem, non tamen necessitans, ut sic potius, quam aliter fiat* (Leibniz, *De libertate*: *Opera*, ed. Erdmann, p. 669).[3] This causes me to observe that such a middle path between the two alternatives above is untenable. We cannot say, according to a certain favorite half-measure, that motives determine the will only up to a certain point; that the will submits to their influence, but only up to a certain degree; and that it can then withdraw from it. For as soon as we have granted causality to a given force, and thus have recognized that it operates, then, in the event of resistance, one need only intensify the force in proportion to it, and it will achieve its effect. Whoever cannot be bribed with ten ducats but yet wavers, will be with a hundred, and so on.

We therefore turn with our problem to immediate *self-consciousness* in the sense that was previously determined by us. Now what disclosure does this self-consciousness give us about that abstract question concerning the applicability or nonapplicability of the concept *necessity* to the occurrence of the act of will subsequent to a given motive, that is, to one that is presented to the intellect? Or about the possibility or impossibility of its failure to occur in such a case? We would be much mistaken if from this self-consciousness we expected thorough and profound disclosures about causality in general and motivation in particular, and also about any necessity attaching to both; for self-consciousness, as found in all human beings, is something much too simple and limited for it to be able to pronounce on such matters. On

---

[1] "On the other hand, we are so thoroughly aware of our freedom and indifference that we do not comprehend anything else so evidently and perfectly" (*Principles of Philosophy*, I, § 41).

[2] Gottfried Wilhelm Leibniz (1646–1716): German philosopher, jurist, and diplomat. The *Essais de Théodicée. Sur la bonté de Dieu, la liberté de l'homme et l'origine du mal* (*Theodicy. On the Goodness of God, the Freedom of the Human Being and the Origin of Evil*) was published in 1710.

[3] "All actions are determined and never indifferent because there always exists a reason which inclines us, although it does not necessarily compel us, to act rather in this way and not in any other" (*On [Human] Freedom*; letter to Coste of 19 December 1707).

the contrary, these concepts are drawn from the outwardly directed pure understanding, and can be discussed only before the tribunal of the faculty of reflective reason. On the other hand, this natural, simple, and indeed plain self-consciousness cannot even understand the question, much less answer it. Its statement about the acts of will, which anyone can hear within his own inner being, may be expressed somewhat as follows, when divested of everything foreign and inessential and reduced to its bare content: "I can will, and when I will an action, the movable limbs of my body will at once and inevitably carry it out the moment I will it." In short, this is equivalent to saying that *"I can do what I will."* The statement of immediate self-consciousness does not go farther than this, no matter how we turn the question or in what form we put it. Its statement therefore always refers to *being able to do in accordance with the will*; but this is the empirical, original, and popular concept of freedom given at the very beginning, according to which *free* means *"in accordance with the will."* Self-consciousness will unconditionally assert this freedom; but it is not that about which we are inquiring. Self-consciousness asserts the freedom of *doing* under the presupposition of *willing*; but what we have inquired about is the freedom of *willing*. For we are asking about the relation between willing itself and the motive; but the statement "I can do what I will" contains nothing about such a relation. The dependence of our doing, that is, of our bodily actions, on our will, which self-consciousness indeed asserts, is something quite different from the independence of our acts of will from external circumstances, which would constitute freedom of the will. On this point, however, self-consciousness cannot state anything, since freedom of the will lies outside its province. For freedom of the will concerns the causal relation of the external world (given to us as the consciousness of other things) to our decisions, but self-consciousness cannot judge of the relation between what lies entirely outside its province and what lies within. For no cognitive power can establish a relation between two things one of which cannot in any way be given to it. But obviously the *objects* of willing, which determine the act of will, lie outside the limit of *self-consciousness*, and are in the consciousness *of other things*. Only the act of will itself is *in* self-consciousness, and we are asking about the causal relation between those outside objects and this act of will. The business of self-consciousness is the act of will alone, together with its absolute mastery over the limbs of the body,

17

which is really meant by the expression "what I will." Even for self-consciousness it is only the exercise of this mastery, i.e., *the deed*, that stamps it as the act of will. For as long as the act of will is in the process of coming about, it is called *wish*; when complete it is called *decision*; but that it is complete is first shown to self-consciousness itself by the *deed*, for until then the decision is changeable. And here we already stand at the chief source of that certainly undeniable illusion by means of which the uninitiated (i.e., the philosophically untutored) imagine that, in a given case, opposite acts of will are possible, and boast of their self-consciousness which, they imagine, asserts this. Thus they confuse wishing with willing; they can *wish* opposite things,[a] but can *will* only one of them; and which one it is is first revealed even to self-consciousness by *the deed*. But as to the necessity according to law whereby one and not the other of two opposite wishes becomes the act of will and deed, self-consciousness cannot contain anything because it learns the result entirely *a posteriori*, but does not know it *a priori*. Opposite wishes with their motives pass up and down before it alternately and repeatedly; about each of them it states that it will become the deed if it becomes the act of will. For this latter purely *subjective* possibility is, to be sure, present for each wish, and is just the "I can do what I will." This *subjective* possibility, however, is entirely hypothetical; it states merely that "*if* I will this, I can *do* it." But the determination requisite for willing does not lie within it; for self-consciousness contains only the willing, not the determining grounds for the willing, which lie in the consciousness of other things, i.e., in the faculty of cognition. On the other hand, it is the *objective* possibility that turns the scale; but the latter lies outside self-consciousness, in the world of objects, to which the motive and the human being as object belong. It is therefore foreign to self-consciousness and belongs to the consciousness of other things. That *subjective* possibility is of the same nature as the possibility of giving sparks which resides in the stone but is conditioned by the steel to which the *objective* possibility adheres. I shall return to this from the other side in the next section, when we consider the will no longer from within, as here, but from without, and hence investigate the *objective* possibility of the act of will. After light

18

---

[a] In this connection see my *Parerga and Paralipomena*, vol. II, § 327 of the first edition.

has been thrown on the matter from two different sides, it will then be quite clear and also be illustrated by examples.

The feeling residing in self-consciousness that "I can do what I will" does constantly accompany us, but states merely that, although the decisions or decided acts of will spring from the dim depths of our inner being, they will always pass over at once into the world of intuition, for our body, like everything else, belongs to that world. This consciousness forms the bridge between the inner and outer worlds that would otherwise remain separated by an insurmountable gap, since in the latter there would then only be intuitions as objects, in every sense independent of us, and in the former nothing but ineffective and merely felt acts of will. – If we were to ask someone who is wholly impartial, he would express somewhat as follows that immediate consciousness which is so frequently taken to be that of a supposed freedom of the will: "I can do what I will; if I want to go to the left, I go to the left; if I want to go to the right, I go to the right. This depends entirely on my will alone; I am therefore free." Certainly this statement is perfectly true and correct, yet with it the will is already presupposed; for it assumes that the will has already made its decision, and hence nothing can be settled thereby concerning the will itself being free. For the statement in no way speaks of the dependence or independence of the *occurrence* of the act of will itself, but only of the *consequences* of this act as soon as it occurs, or, to speak more accurately, of the act's inevitable appearance as bodily action. But it is simply and solely the consciousness underlying that statement which causes the naive, i.e., the philosophically untutored human being, who in spite of this may yet be a great scholar in other disciplines, to regard the freedom of the will as something so absolutely and immediately certain that he expresses it as an unquestionable truth, and really cannot believe that philosophers seriously doubt it, but thinks in his heart that all the talk about it is mere dialectical school-fencing and at bottom play. Now the undoubtedly important certainty given by that con-sciousness is always quite close at hand; moreover the human being, as primarily and essentially a practical and not a theoretical being, is much more clearly conscious of the active side of his acts of will, i.e., of their effectiveness, than of the *passive*, i.e., of their dependence. For this reason, it is so difficult to make the human being who is philosophically untrained understand the real meaning of our problem, and to get him

19

to see that the question is now not one of the *consequences* but of the *grounds* of his willing in each case. It is true that his *action* depends simply and solely on his *willing*, but we now want to know on what *his willing itself* depends, if on nothing at all or on something. He can certainly *do* one thing if he wants to, and can just as well *do* the other thing if he wants to; but he should now ask himself whether he is also capable of *willing* one thing as well as the other. Now with this object in view, let us put the question to the human being in some such terms as the following: "Of two opposite wishes that have arisen in you, can you really satisfy the one as well as the other? For example, when choosing between two mutually exclusive objects, can you prefer the possession of the one just as well as that of the other?" He will then say: "Perhaps the choice may be difficult for me, yet it will always depend entirely on me whether I *will* to choose the one or the other, and will not depend on any other authority; for I have complete freedom to choose what I *will*, and here I shall always follow only my *will*." – Now if we say to him: "But on what does your willing itself depend?" he will reply out of his self-consciousness: "On absolutely nothing but me! I can will what I will; what I will that I will." – The latter he says without meaning to be tautological, or without relying in his inmost consciousness on the principle of identity by virtue of which alone this is true. On the contrary, when pressed to the very limit here, he speaks of a willing of his willing, which is as if he were to speak of an I of his I. He has been driven back to the very core of his self-consciousness, where he finds his I and his will to be indistinguishable, but nothing is left for assessing the two. Whether in that choice his *willing itself* of one thing and not of the other, for his person and the objects of choice are here assumed as given, could possibly turn out differently from what it ultimately does; or whether, by the data just mentioned, it is determined just as necessarily as that in a triangle the greatest angle is subtended by the greatest side – this is a question so remote from natural *self-consciousness* that it cannot even understand it, much less have a ready answer for it, or even only the undeveloped germ of one, which it could give out only naively. – Therefore in the way just indicated, the impartial but philosophically untutored human being will still always try to run away from the perplexity that the question, when really understood, is bound to cause, and will take refuge behind that immediate certainty "what I will I can do, and I will what I will," as

20

was said above. He will attempt to do this over and over again innumerable times, so that it will be difficult to pin him down to the real question from which he is always trying to slip away. And for this he is not to be blamed, for the question is really extremely ticklish. It thrusts a searching hand into the inmost recesses of the human being; it wants to know whether he too, like everything else in the world, is a being once and for all determined by its own constitution; a being, like every other in nature, having its definite constant qualities from which there necessarily spring its reactions to the external occasion that arises and which accordingly, from this point of view, bear their unalterable character, and consequently are wholly abandoned, in whatever may be modifiable in them, to determination by occasion from without; or whether he alone is an exception to the whole of nature. If, however, we finally succeed in pinning him down to this so ticklish question, and in making it clear to him that we are here inquiring about the origin of his acts of will themselves, and are asking whether they arise in accordance with some rule or entirely without any, we shall discover that immediate self-consciousness contains no information about this. For the untutored human being himself here departs from self-consciousness and reveals his perplexity through speculation and all kinds of attempted explanations. He tries to draw the arguments for them at first from the experience he has acquired of himself and others, and then from universal rules of the understanding. But through the uncertainty and hesitancy of his explanation he here shows plainly enough that his immediate self-consciousness furnishes no information about the question when correctly understood, although previously it was ready with an answer when the question was incorrectly understood. Ultimately, this is due to the fact that the will of the human being is his real self, the true kernel of his being; it therefore constitutes the ground of his consciousness, as something absolutely given and existing beyond which he cannot go. For he himself is as he wills, and he wills as he is. Therefore to ask him whether he could will otherwise than he does is tantamount to asking him whether he could be different from what he himself is; and this he does not know. For the same reason if the philosopher, who differs from the ordinary human being only through training, is to see his way clearly in this difficult matter, he must turn to his understanding, which furnishes cognitions *a priori*, to his faculty of reason, which reflects on the latter, and to experience, which brings his own actions and those of others to him for interpretation and control by the cognition of the understanding; to these he must turn as the final and only competent tribunal. It is true that the decision of this court will not be so easy, immediate, and simple as that of self-consciousness, but for all that it will be appropriate to the matter and adequate. The head has posed the question and must also answer it.

Meanwhile it must not surprise us that immediate self-consciousness has no answer to offer to this abstruse, speculative, difficult, and ticklish question. For it is a very limited part of our total consciousness, which, obscure within, is directed with all its objective cognitive powers entirely outward. All its perfectly certain, i.e., *a priori* certain, cognitions concern the external world alone, and there it can positively decide, according to certain universal laws rooted in itself, what is possible, impossible, and necessary out there. In this way it brings about *a priori* pure mathematics, pure logic, even pure fundamental natural science. Accordingly the application of its forms (known to it *a priori*) to the data given in sensation furnishes it with intuition of the real external world and hence with experience. Further, the application of logic and of the thinking faculty underlying the latter will furnish for that external world concepts, the world of thoughts, thus in turn the sciences, their achievements, and so on. Therefore great brightness and clarity are there for it to see *outside*; but *inside* it is dark, like a well-blackened telescope. No principle *a priori* illuminates the night of its own interior; these lighthouses shine only outward. As previously discussed, there exists for the so-called inner sense nothing but our own will to whose movements all the so-called inner feelings are actually traceable. But all that is furnished by this inner perception of the will goes back, as I have shown above, to willing and not-willing together with the lauded certainty that "I can *do* what I *will*." This really states that "I see at once every act of my will (in a way quite incomprehensible to me) manifesting itself as an action of my body" – and, strictly speaking, it is for the knowing subject an empirical proposition. Beyond this nothing can be found here. The tribunal to which the question is brought is, therefore, incompetent to settle it; indeed, in its true form the question cannot be brought at all before this tribunal, for it does not understand it.

I now sum up once more in shorter and easier terms the answer to our inquiry which we obtained from self-consciousness. Everyone's *self-consciousness* very clearly states that he can do what he wills. Now since entirely opposite actions can be conceived as *willed* by him, it certainly follows that he can also do the opposite, *if he wills*. Now the untrained understanding confuses this with the statement that, in a given case, he can also *will* the opposite, and calls this *the freedom of the will*. But in the statement above there is absolutely nothing to the effect that, in a given case, he can *will* the opposite. On the contrary, it says merely that of two opposite actions he can do this if he *wills it*, and can likewise do that if he *wills it*; but whether in the given case he *can will* the one as well as the other remains undecided. This is the subject of a deeper investigation than can be settled by mere self-consciousness. For this result the shortest formula, although scholastic, would say that the statement of self-consciousness concerns the will merely *a parte post*, but the question regarding freedom concerns it *a parte ante*.[4] – Therefore that undeniable statement of self-consciousness that "I can do what I will" contains and settles absolutely nothing about the freedom of the will. Such freedom would exist if the particular act of will itself in a particular individual case, and hence with a given individual character, were necessarily determined not by the external circumstances in which that human being happened to be, but could now turn out thus and also otherwise. But on this point self-consciousness remains completely silent, for the matter lies entirely outside its province, depending as it does on the causal relation between the external world and the human being. If we ask a human being of ordinary common sense, but without any philosophical education, in what the freedom of the will consists, a freedom so confidently maintained by him in the statement of his self-consciousness, he will answer that it consists "in my being able to do what I will, the moment I am not physically checked." Thus it is always the relation of his *doing* to his *willing* about which he speaks. But, as was shown in the first section, this is still only *physical* freedom. If we then ask him further whether in the given case he can *will* one thing as well as its opposite, he will hastily answer in the affirmative; but as soon as he begins to grasp the meaning of the question, he will also begin to hesitate and will become uncertain and confused. From this confusion he will again take refuge behind his favorite theme "I can do what I will," and will

24

[4] *A parte post*: "with regard to what follows"; *a parte ante*: "with regard to what precedes."

there entrench himself against all argument and reasoning. But, as I hope to put beyond all doubt in the following section, the corrected answer to his theme would be: "You can *do* what you *will*, but at any given moment of your life you can *will* only one definite thing and absolutely nothing else but this one thing."

Now the question of the Royal Society would really be answered, and in fact in the negative, by the discussion contained in this section, although only in the main, since this exposition of the state of affairs in self-consciousness will be rendered even more complete by what follows. But now in *one* case there is even a check for this negative answer of ours. Thus if we now turn with our question to that authority to which, as the only competent one, we were previously referred, namely to the pure understanding, to the faculty of reason reflecting on the latter's data, and to experience which results from both, and if their decision proved to be that a *liberum arbitrium* in general did not exist, but that human conduct, like everything else in nature, in every given case ensued as a necessarily occurring effect, then this would give us the assurance that in immediate self-consciousness *there could not possibly be found* data from which the *liberum arbitrium* we are inquiring about could be established. In this way, by means of the conclusion *a non posse ad non esse*,[5] which is the only possible way to establish *negative a priori* truths, our decision would obtain a rational foundation in addition to the empirical one hitherto provided, and would then in consequence be made doubly sure. For we cannot accept as possible a final contradiction between the immediate utterances of self-consciousness and the results from the fundamental principles of the pure understanding together with their application to experience; ours cannot be so mendacious a self-consciousness. It must be observed here that even the alleged antinomy advanced by *Kant* on this topic[6] is not supposed to result, even for him, from the thesis and antithesis coming from different sources of cognition, one possibly from the utterances of self-consciousness, and the other from the faculty of reason and experience. On the contrary, thesis and antithesis both rationalize from allegedly objective grounds. However, the thesis relies on absolutely nothing but indolent reason, i.e., on the need for standing still at some

25

---

[5] "From what cannot be to what is not."   [6] See *Critique of Pure Reason*, A 444ff./B 472ff.

point in the regress; the antithesis, on the other hand, really has in its favor all the objective grounds.

Accordingly, that *indirect* investigation now to be made, which is carried out in the province of the faculty of cognition and of the external world before it, will at the same time throw much light on the *direct* one hitherto carried out, and will thus serve to supplement it. For it will disclose the natural deceptions that result from the false interpretation of that extremely simple utterance of self-consciousness, when the latter comes into conflict with the consciousness of other things, or the faculty of cognition which is rooted in one and the same subject with self-consciousness. In fact, only at the conclusion of this indirect investigation will some light dawn on us concerning the true meaning and content of that "I will" which accompanies all our actions, and concerning the consciousness of an original and spontaneous nature by virtue of which they are *our* actions. Only in this way will the direct investigation carried out so far become complete.

26

III
The will before the consciousness of other things

If with our problem we now turn to the faculty of cognition, we know in advance that, since that faculty is directed essentially outward, the will cannot be for it an object of immediate perception as it was for self-consciousness, which was nevertheless deemed to be incompetent in this matter. On the contrary, we know that here only *beings* endowed with a will can be considered, which stand before the faculty of cognition as objective and external appearances, i.e., as objects of experience, and are now to be examined and judged as such, partly according to universal *a priori* certain rules that are established for experience in general with respect to the latter's possibility, and partly in accordance with the facts that are furnished by complete and actual experience. Thus here we are no longer concerned, as previously, with the *will* itself as revealed only to the inner sense, but with the willing *beings moved by the will*, who are objects of the outer senses. Although we are placed at the disadvantage now of having to consider the proper object of our inquiry only mediately and at a greater distance, this is outweighed by the advantage of our being able in our investigation now to make use of a much more perfect organon than the dim, dull, one-sided, direct self-consciousness, the so-called inner sense. Thus we have the advantage of using the *understanding* which is equipped with all the outer senses and powers for *objective* apprehension.

We find the *law of causality* as the most universal and fundamentally essential form of this understanding, for by means of it alone the intuition of the real external world is brought about, in that we apprehend the affections and changes felt in our sense organs at once and quite immediately as "*effects*." Without guidance, instruction, and experience we pass instantaneously from these to their "*causes*," which present themselves through this very process of the understanding as *objects in space.*[a] From this it is incontestably clear that the *law of causality* is known to us *a priori* and consequently as a *necessary* law as regards the possibility of all experience in general. We do not need for this important truth the indirect, difficult, and in fact insufficient proof given by *Kant*. The law of causality stands firm *a priori* as the universal rule to which all the real objects of the external world are subject without exception. It owes this absence of exception to its *a priori* nature. The law refers essentially and exclusively to *changes*, and states that wherever and whenever in the objective, real, material world anything, great or small, much or little, *changes*, necessarily something else must have *changed* just *previously*; for *this* something to *change*, there must have been again another *before it*, and so on to infinity. In this regressive series of changes, which fills time just as matter fills space, no initial point can be seen or even conceived as possible, much less presupposed. For the question persistently cropping up "what produced this change?" never allows the understanding a final resting-point, however weary of this regressus it may grow. For this reason, a first cause is just as unthinkable as is a beginning in time or a limit to space. – The law of causality likewise states that when the earlier change, *the cause*, has occurred, the latter change thereby produced, *the effect*, must occur quite inevitably and consequently ensues *necessarily*. Through this character of *necessity* the law of causality proves to be a form of the *principle of sufficient reason*. This principle is the most universal form of our whole faculty of cognition, and just as it appears in the real world as causality, so in the world of thought it appears as the logical law of the ground of cognition. Even in empty, but *a priori* intuited, space it appears as the law of the strictly necessary dependence of the position of all its parts on one another, the sole theme of geometry being the special and detailed demonstration of this necessary dependence. And so, as I discussed already at the beginning, *being necessary* and *being the consequent of a given ground* are convertible concepts.

All *changes* that occur in given objects in the real external world are therefore subject to the law of *causality*, and thus always occur as

28

---

[a] A thorough discussion of this doctrine is found in the treatise *On the Fourfold Root of the Principle of Sufficient Reason*, § 21 of the second edition.

necessary and inevitable, whenever and wherever they occur. – To this law there can be no exception, for the rule holds *a priori* for all possibility of experience. But as regards its *application* to a given case, we have merely to ask whether we are dealing with a *change* of a real object that is given in external experience. When this is so, its changes are subject to the application of the law of causality; in other words, they must be brought about by a cause, and for that very reason must *necessarily* be brought about.

If we now approach this experience itself with our universal, *a priori* certain rule, which is therefore valid without exception for all possible experience, and consider the real objects given in experience to whose possible changes our rule refers, we soon notice in those objects some fundamentally striking main differences in accordance with which they also have long been classified. Thus some objects are inorganic, i.e., inanimate; others are organic, i.e., animate, and the latter again are either plants or animals. Animals again, although essentially similar and conforming to their concept, are still found in an extremely varied and finely shaded hierarchy of perfection, from those still closely akin to a plant, and hardly distinguishable from it, up to those that are most perfect and conform most perfectly to the concept of an animal. At the summit of this hierarchy we see the human being – ourselves.

Now if, without allowing ourselves to be confused by that multiplicity and variety, we consider all those beings together merely as external, real objects of experience, and accordingly proceed to apply to the changes occurring in such beings our law of causality that stands *a priori* firm for the possibility of all experience, we shall find that experience certainly does turn out everywhere in accordance with the *a priori* certain law, yet to the mentioned great *diversity* in the essential nature of all those objects of experience there also corresponds a modification, appropriate to that diversity, of the way in which causality asserts its right in them. Thus, in keeping with the threefold distinction of inorganic bodies, plants, and animals, causality that guides and directs all their changes likewise shows itself in three forms, as *cause* in the narrowest sense of the word, or as *stimulus*, or as *motivation*; and yet this modification does not in the least detract from the *a priori* validity of causality and consequently from the necessity, thereby established, with which the effect follows the cause.

Cause in the narrowest sense of the word is that by virtue of which all mechanical, physical, and chemical changes occur in the objects of experience. It is everywhere characterized by two distinctive features; first by the fact that Newton's third law that "action and reaction are equal" finds its application here; in other words, the antecedent state, called cause, undergoes a change equal to that undergone by the ensuing state, called the effect. – Secondly, cause in the narrowest sense is characterized by the fact that, according to Newton's second law, the degree of the effect is always exactly proportionate to that of the cause; consequently an intensification of the cause likewise brings about an equal intensification of the effect. Thus once the mode of operation is known, the degree of the effect can also be known, measured, and calculated at once from the degree of the intensity of the cause, and vice versa. But in the empirical application of this second distinctive feature we must not confuse the effect proper with its visible appearance. For example, in the compression of a body we must not expect its volume to be constantly decreased in proportion as the compressing force is increased. For the space into which the body is compressed is always decreasing, and consequently the resistance increases; and although the effect proper here, namely the increase in density, does actually grow in proportion to the cause, as Mariotte's law states, this cannot be understood from its visible phenomenon. Moreover, in many cases, at certain and definite degrees of pressure, the whole mode of efficacy will change all at once because actually the mode of counteraction changes, since its mode up to that moment has been exhausted in a body of finite size. For example, heat conducted to water will raise its temperature to a certain degree, but beyond this it will produce only rapid evaporation; but here again the same relation comes in between the degree of the cause and that of the effect; and so it is in many cases. Now it is such *causes in the narrowest sense* that produce the changes in all *inanimate, i.e., inorganic* bodies. The cognition and presupposition of causes of this kind guide our consideration of all the changes that form the subject of mechanics, hydrodynamics, physics, and chemistry. To be determined exclusively by causes of this kind is, therefore, the proper and essential characteristic of an inorganic or inanimate body.

The second kind of causes is *stimulus*, i.e., that cause which in the first place does *not* itself undergo a reaction proportionate to its action; and, in the second place, that in which there is absolutely no uniformity between the intensity of the cause and that of the effect. Consequently,

30

the degree of the effect here cannot be measured and previously determined in accordance with that of the cause. On the contrary, a small increase in the stimulus may cause a very great increase in the effect; or conversely it may eliminate the previous effect entirely, or even bring about an opposite one. For example, it is well known that plants can be forced to an extraordinarily rapid growth by heat or the addition of lime to the soil, because those causes act as stimuli to the plants' vital force. If, however, the appropriate degree of stimulus is very minutely exceeded, then, instead of an enhanced and quickened life, the result will be the death of the plant. Thus we can also exert and considerably heighten our mental powers by wine or opium, but if the right amount of stimulus is exceeded, the result will be the very opposite. – It is causes of this kind, namely *stimuli*, that determine all the changes of organisms *as such*. All the changes and developments of plants and all the merely organic and vegetative changes or functions of animal bodies occur through *stimuli*. Light, heat, air, nutrition, every drug, touch, fructification, and so on act on them in this way. – But the life of animals still has quite a different sphere, about which I shall speak in a moment; the entire life of *plants* takes place exclusively in accordance with *stimuli*. All their assimilation, growth, the striving of their crowns to reach the light and of their roots toward the better soil, their fructification, germination, and so on are changes brought about by *stimuli*. In a few isolated species there is also a characteristic swift movement that is likewise solely the result of stimuli, and for this reason they are called sensitive plants. The best-known of these are *Mimosa pudica*, *Hedysarum gyrans*, and *Dionaea muscipula*.[1] To be determined by *stimuli* exclusively and without exception is the character of the plant. Consequently, a plant is any body whose movements and changes peculiar and appropriate to its nature always and exclusively follow on *stimuli*.

The third kind of moving cause, which characterizes *animals*, is *motivation*, i.e., causality that passes through *cognition*. It enters in the gradual scale of natural beings at that point where a being which is more complex, and thus has more manifold needs, was no longer able

31

---

[1] *Mimosa pudica* or "sensitive plant" is a tropical American plant whose leaves are sensitive to tactile stimulation. *Hedysarum gyrans*, a tropical Asian plant whose leaves rotate slowly but visibly in daylight at temperatures above 72 °F, has been reclassified at least twice since the nineteenth century, most recently as *Codariocalyx motorius*. The English name of the plant is "telegraph plant" or "semaphore plant." *Dionaea muscipula* is the familiar Venus's-flytrap.

to satisfy them merely on the occasion of a stimulus that must be awaited, but had to be in a position to choose, seize, and even seek out the means of satisfaction. And so with beings of this kind, mere susceptibility to *stimuli* and movement therefrom are replaced by susceptibility to *motives*, i.e., by a faculty of representation, an intellect in innumerable degrees of perfection. This manifests itself materially as a nervous system and brain and thus entails consciousness. It is well known that the basis of animal life is a plant life that as such takes place only on *stimuli*. But all movements performed by an animal *as an animal*, and hence depending on what physiology calls *animal functions*, occur in consequence of a known object, and hence *on motives*. Accordingly, an *animal* is any body whose external movements and changes, peculiar and appropriate to its nature, always ensue *on motives*, i.e., on certain *representations* that are present to its here already presupposed consciousness. However infinite graduations there may be of the capacity for representations and thus for consciousness in the series of animals, there is nevertheless in every animal enough of it for the motives to present itself to it and cause it to move. Here the inner moving force whose particular manifestation is called forth by the motive proclaims itself to the now existing self-consciousness as that which we denote by the word *will*.

Now the mode of efficacy of a stimulus is so obviously different from that of a motive that even for observation from without, which is here our standpoint, there can never be any doubt whether a given body is moved by *stimuli* or *motives*. For a stimulus acts always through immediate contact or even by being absorbed; and even where the latter is not visible, such as when the stimulus is air, light, or heat, it nevertheless reveals itself by the fact that the effect has an unmistakable relation to the duration and intensity of the stimulus, even though this relation does not remain the same with all degrees of the stimulus. On the other hand, where a *motive* causes the movement, all such distinctions entirely disappear. For here the proper and proximate medium of the influence is not the atmosphere, but simply *cognition*. The object acting as motive needs only to be *perceived* or *cognized*. Here it is immaterial how long, whether near or remote, and how clearly it has entered apperception. Here all such distinctions do not in the least alter the degree of the effect; as soon as it has been perceived, it acts in exactly the same way, provided that it is at all a determining ground of the will that is to be stirred here. For physical and chemical causes, also stimuli, likewise act only insofar as the body to be affected is *susceptible* to them. I said just now "the will that is to be stirred here"; for, as already mentioned, that which properly imparts to the motive the power to act, the secret spring of the motion that is produced by the motive, proclaims itself inwardly and immediately here to the being itself as that which is denoted by the word *will*. In the case of bodies moving exclusively through a stimulus (plants), we call that constant inner condition vital force; – with those bodies that move merely through causes in the narrowest sense, we call it natural force or quality. Explanations always presuppose it as the inexplicable, since inside the beings there is no self-consciousness here to which it would be immediately accessible. Now if we leave *the appearance in general* and wish to inquire about what Kant calls the thing in itself, there is the question whether the inner condition of reaction to external causes in the case of beings without cognition and even without life is essentially identical with what we call the *will* in ourselves, as a philosopher of recent times actually sought to demonstrate to us. I leave this point undecided without, however, wishing to contradict this directly.[b]

On the other hand, I cannot omit discussing the difference brought about in motivation by that which distinguishes human consciousness from all animal consciousness. This trait, which is properly expressed by the word *reason*, consists in a human being not merely capable, like an animal, of an *intuitive* apprehension of the external world, but also of abstracting universal concepts (*notiones universales*) from it. To be able to fix and retain these in his sensuous consciousness, he denotes them by words, and then makes innumerable combinations with them. These, like the concepts of which they consist, are of course related always to the world that is known through intuition, yet they properly constitute what we call *thinking*. The great advantages of the human species over all the rest thus become possible, such as speech, reflectiveness, looking back at the past, care about the future, purpose, deliberation, the planned and systematic action of many in common, the state, the sciences, the arts, and so on. All this rests solely on the unique ability to have nonintuitive, abstract, universal representations, called

34

[b] Here, of course, I am speaking of myself, and only because of the required incognito was it not possible for me to speak in the first person.

concepts (i.e., conceptual complexes of things),[2] because each of them contains or comprehends under itself many particular things. Animals, even the cleverest, lack this ability, and therefore have no other representations than *intuitive representations*. Accordingly, they know only what is actually present, and live solely in the present moment. The motives by which their will is moved must therefore always be intuitive and present. But the result of this is that an exceedingly limited *choice* is granted to them, namely only among those things which are present in intuition for their limited range of view and power of apprehension and thus are present in time and space. The stronger of these then at once determines their will as motive, whereby the causality of the motive here becomes very obvious. An *apparent* exception is made by *training*, which is fear operating through the medium of habit. But instinct is to a certain extent a *real* exception insofar as, by reason of it, the animal is set into motion in the *whole* of its mode of action not by motives proper, but by an inner urge and drive. But in the details of the *particular* actions and at every moment the latter receives again its closer determination through motives, and thus returns to the rule. A more detailed discussion of instinct would take me too far from my theme; chapter 27 of the second volume of my main work is devoted to it. – On the other hand, owing to his capacity for *nonintuitive* representations, by means of which he *thinks and reflects*, a human being has an infinitely wider range of view, which encompasses the absent, the past, and the future. He thus has a far greater sphere of influence of motives and consequently also of choice than an animal has, restricted as it is to the narrowness of the present moment. As a rule, it is not the thing lying before his sensible intuition and present in time and space which determines his action, but rather mere *thoughts*, which he carries about in his head wherever he goes, and which make him independent of the impression of the present moment. Whenever the latter fail to do this, however, we call his conduct irrational; on the other hand, his conduct is commended as *rational* when it takes place exclusively according to well-considered thoughts, and thus quite independently of the impression of what is present in intuition. A human being is actuated by a special class of representations (abstract concepts, thoughts), which an animal does not have, and this is evident

35

---

[2] The German words are "Begriffe" and "Inbegriffe der Dinge," respectively.

even externally; for this circumstance impresses the character of the *deliberate and intentional* on all his actions, even the most insignificant, in fact on all his steps and movements. Thus his whole line of conduct is so obviously different from that of animals that one almost sees how, as it were, fine, invisible threads (motives consisting of mere thoughts) guide his movements, whereas those of animals are drawn by the coarse, visible ropes of what is present in intuition. But the difference does not go beyond this. A thought becomes *motive*, as does an intuition, as soon as it is able to act on the will that lies before it. But all motives are causes, and all causality entails necessity. Now by means of his ability to think, a human being can represent to himself the motives whose influence he feels on his will in any order he likes, alternately and repeatedly, in order to hold them before the will; and this is called *reflecting*. He has a capacity for deliberation and, by virtue of it, a far greater *choice* than is possible for the animal. In this way, he certainly is *relatively free*, namely from the immediate compulsion of objects that are *present through intuition* and act as motives on his will, a compulsion to which the animal is absolutely subject. A human being, on the other hand, determines himself independently of present objects, in accordance with thoughts, which are *his* motives. At bottom it is this *relative* freedom that educated but not deep-thinking people understand by freedom of the will, which, they say, obviously gives the human being the advantage over the animal. But such freedom is merely *relative*, namely in reference to what is present through intuition, and merely *comparative*, namely in comparison with the *animal*. Only *the mode* of motivation is changed by it; on the other hand, the *necessity* of the effect of the motives is not in the least suspended or even only diminished. The *abstract* motive that consists in a mere *thought* is an external cause determining the will just as is the intuitive motive, which consists in a real object that is present. Consequently, it is a cause like every other and is even, like other causes, at all times something real and material insofar as it always rests ultimately on an impression received *from without* at some time and place. Its advantage lies merely in the length of the guiding wire. By this I mean that it is not, like the merely intuitive motives, bound to a certain *proximity* in space and time, but can operate through the greatest distance and longest time by means of concepts and thoughts in a long concatenation. This is a consequence of the constitution and eminent susceptibility of the organ which first experiences and receives its impression, namely the human brain or *reason*. But this does not in the least suspend its causality and the *necessity* associated with it. Therefore only a very superficial view can regard that relative and comparative freedom as absolute, as a *liberum arbitrium indifferentiae*. Indeed, the capacity for deliberation, arising from that comparative freedom, gives us nothing but a *conflict of motives*, one that is very often painful, over which irresolution presides, and whose scene of conflict is the whole mind and consciousness of the human being. For he allows the motives repeatedly to try their strength on his will, one against the other. His will is thus put in the same position as that of a body that is acted on by different forces in opposite directions – until at last the decidedly strongest motive drives the others from the field and determines the will. This outcome is called decision and, as the result of the struggle, appears with complete *necessity*.

Now if we review once more the whole series of the forms of causality in which *causes* in the narrowest sense of the word, then *stimuli*, and finally *motives* are clearly separated from one another, and motives in turn are divided into intuitive and abstract ones, we shall observe, as we go through the series of beings in this respect from below upward, that the cause and its effect become ever more widely separated, more clearly differentiated, and more heterogeneous from each other. In particular, the cause becomes less and less material and palpable, and thus less and less appears to lie in the cause and more and more in the effect. The result of all this is that the connection between cause and effect loses its immediate comprehensibility and intelligibility. Thus all that has just been said is to the least extent the case with *mechanical* causality, which is therefore the *most comprehensible* of all. From this there arose in the preceding century the false attempt, still maintained in France but also recently taken up in Germany, to reduce every other kind of causality to this, to explain all physical and chemical processes from mechanical causes, and then to explain from those processes the vital process. The impinging body moves the one at rest, and imparts as much motion as it loses; here we see the cause, as it were, passing over into the effect; both are quite homogeneous, exactly commensurable, and moreover palpable; and this is really the case with all purely mechanical effects. But we shall find that, the higher we go, all this is less and less the case, and rather what was previously said becomes relevant. Thus let us consider at each stage the relation between cause and effect, for instance, between heat as cause and its various effects such as expansion, incandescence, fusion, volatilization, combustion, thermoelectricity, and so on; or between evaporation as cause and cooling or crystallization as effects; or between the rubbing of glass as cause and free electricity with its strange phenomena as effect; or between the slow oxidation of the plates as cause and galvanism with all its electrical, chemical, and magnetic phenomena as effect. Thus cause and effect are ever more *separated* and become *more heterogeneous*; their connection becomes *less intelligible*. The effect appears to contain more than could be imparted to it by the cause, for the latter appears to be less and less material and palpable. All this becomes even plainer when we pass to *organic* bodies, where the causes are now mere *stimuli*, partly external, such as those of light, heat, air, soil, nutrition, and partly internal, such as those of the humors and parts stimulating one another, and their effect manifests itself as life with its infinite complexity and countless varieties of species, as seen in the manifold forms of the plant and animal kingdoms.[c]

But now in this ever-increasing heterogeneity, incommensurability, and incomprehensibility of the relation between cause and effect, has the *necessity* laid down by the relation in any way diminished? Not in the very least. Just as the rolling ball necessarily sets in motion the one at rest, so too must the Leyden jar just as necessarily discharge itself on contact with the other hand, so too must arsenic kill every living thing, so also must the seed, which when kept dry showed no change throughout thousands of years, germinate, grow, and develop into a plant as soon as it is put into suitable soil and exposed to the influence of air, light, heat, and moisture. The cause is more complex, the effect more heterogeneous, but the necessity with which it enters is not less by a hair's breadth.

In the life of the plant and the vegetative life of the animal, the stimulus is, of course, very different in every respect from the organic function that is thereby produced, and the two are distinctly separated; yet they are not properly *detached*, but between them there must exist a contact, however slight and invisible. Total separation first appears in animal life, whose actions are called forth by motives. In this way, the

[c] The more detailed discussion of this separation of cause and effect from each other is found in my *On the Will in Nature* under the heading "Physical Astronomy."

cause, hitherto still materially connected with the effect, now stands completely detached from it, is of quite a different nature and something primarily immaterial, a mere representation. And so in the *motive* that calls forth the animal's movement all these reach the highest degree: that heterogeneity between cause and effect, the severance of the two from each other, their incommensurability, the immateriality of the cause and hence its apparently containing not enough in comparison with the effect. The incomprehensibility of the relation between cause and effect would become absolute if we knew this causal relation, like all others, merely *from without*. But here external cognition is supplemented by one of quite a different kind, by internal cognition, and the process that takes place here as effect after the cause has entered is intimately known to us; we express it by a *terminus ad hoc*, namely will. But we state that here too, as previously with the stimulus, the causal relation has lost nothing of its *necessity*, the moment we recognize it as a *causal relation*, and think through this form which is essential to our understanding. Moreover we find motivation to be wholly analogous to the two other forms of the causal relation previously discussed, and to be merely the highest stage to which these are raised by a very gradual transition. At the lowest stages of animal life the *motive* is still closely akin to the *stimulus*; zoophytes, radiata in general, acephala among the molluscs, have only a feeble glimmer of consciousness, just enough for them to perceive their food or prey and seize it when it presents itself, and perhaps to exchange their locality for one more favorable. At these low stages, therefore, the effect of the motive still lies before us just as distinctly, immediately, decidedly, and unambiguously as does that of the stimulus. Small insects are drawn into the flame by the shining light; flies settle confidently on the head of the lizard that has just swallowed before their eyes others of their kind. Who will dream here of freedom? In the higher and more intelligent animals the effect of the motives becomes more and more indirect. Thus the motive is more distinctly separated from the action produced thereby, so that one could even use this difference of distance between motive and action as a measure of the intelligence of animals. In the human being this distance becomes immeasurable. On the other hand, even in the cleverest animals the representation that becomes the motive of their actions must still always be an *intuitive one*. Even where a choice becomes possible, this can take place only between things that are present in intuition. The dog stands hesitating between the call of his master and the sight of a bitch; the stronger motive will determine his movement; but the latter then ensues just as necessarily as does a mechanical effect. Even in the latter case we see a body put out of equilibrium oscillate for a time from side to side, until it is decided on which its center of gravity lies, and it falls on that side. Now as long as motivation is limited to *intuitive* representations, its affinity with the stimulus and the cause in general is further obvious from the fact that the motive as the effective cause must be something real and present; in fact it must still act physically on the senses, although very indirectly, through light, sound, and odor. Moreover here the cause lies before the observer just as plainly and openly as does the effect. He sees the motive enter and the animal's action ensue inevitably, as long as no other equally obvious motive or training act against it. It is impossible to doubt the connection between the two. Hence it will not occur to anyone to attribute to animals a *liberum arbitrium indifferentiae*, that is to say, an action determined by no cause.

But now where consciousness is rational and hence capable of nonintuitive cognition, i.e., concepts and thoughts, the motives become quite independent of the present moment and of the real environment, and thus remain hidden from the spectator. For now they are mere thoughts carried round by the human being in his head, yet their origin lies outside the head and often very far away. Thus they may lie in his own experience of past years, or in some tradition handed down orally and in writing by others, even from the earliest times, yet such that their *origin is always real and objective*, although, through the often difficult combination of complex external circumstances, many errors and delusions due to transmission, and consequently many follies as well, are among the motives. Added to this is the fact that a human being often conceals the motives of his actions from everyone else, and sometimes even from himself, namely where he shrinks from acknowledging what it really is that moves him to do this or that. Meanwhile we see his actions ensue, and try by conjectures to ascertain the motives; for here we assume these just as firmly and confidently as we do the cause of every motion of inanimate bodies which we have seen ensue. We assume this, convinced as we are that the one, like the other, is impossible without a cause. Conversely, in our own plans and undertakings, we also take into account the effect of motives on human

40

41

35

beings with an assurance that would rival that with which we calculate the effects of mechanical contrivances, if only we knew the individual characters of the human beings with whom we have to deal as exactly as the length and thickness of the beams, the diameter of the wheels, the amount of the loads, and so on. This assumption is observed by everyone as long as he looks outward, deals with others, and pursues practical ends; for the human understanding is destined to such ends. But if he tries to judge the matter theoretically and philosophically – to which human intelligence is not really destined – and now makes himself the object of his judgment, then he may be led astray by the previously described immaterial nature of abstract motives, that consist of mere thoughts, since they are not tied to any present moment and environment and find again their hindrances only in mere thoughts as countermotives. Thus he may be so led astray as to doubt their existence or indeed the necessity of their efficacy, and to imagine that what is done can just as well be left undone; that the will decides by itself without cause; and that each of its acts was a first beginning of an immensely long series of changes produced by that act. Now that error is specially reinforced by the false interpretation of that statement of self-consciousness: "I can do what I will," which was sufficiently investigated in the first section, and this is especially the case if this statement makes itself heard where there are, as always, several motives that merely solicit for the time being and mutually exclude one another. All this taken together is therefore the source of that natural deception from which springs the error that in our self-consciousness lies the certainty of a freedom of our will in the sense that, contrary to all the laws of the pure understanding and of nature, the will determines itself without sufficient reasons, and that under given circumstances its decisions could turn out thus or even in the opposite way in the case of one and the same human being.

42 To render as clearly as possible the origin of that error which is so important to our theme, and thus to supplement the investigation of self-consciousness that was given in the preceding section, let us think of a man in the street who says to himself: "It is six o'clock; the day's work is over. I can now go for a walk, or go to the club; I can also climb the tower to see the sun set; I can also go to the theater; I can also visit this or that friend; in fact I can also run out by the city gate into the wide world and never come back. All that is entirely up to me; I have

complete freedom; however, I do none of them, but just as voluntarily go home to my wife." This is just as if water were to say: "I can form high waves (as in a storm at sea); I can rush down a hill (as in the bed of a torrent); I can dash down foaming and splashing (as in the waterfall); I can rise freely as a jet into the air (as in a fountain); finally, I can even boil away and disappear (as at 212 degrees Fahrenheit); however, I do none of these things now, but voluntarily remain calm and clear in the mirroring pond." Just as water can do all those things only when the determining causes enter for one or the other, so is the condition just the same for that man with respect to what he imagines he can do. Until the causes enter, it is impossible for him to do anything; but then he *must* do it, just as water must act as soon as it is placed in the respective circumstances. When the matter is closely considered, his error and the deception in general which arises from the wrongly interpreted self-consciousness that he is now equally capable of doing all those things are due to the fact that only *one* image at a time can be present in his imagination and that for the moment this image excludes all others. Now if he pictures to himself the motive for one of those actions that are suggested as possible, he at once feels its effect on his will that is thus solicited. In technical language this is called a *velleitas*;[3] but now he thinks he can raise the latter to a *voluntas*,[4] i.e., carry out the proposed action; but this is a deception. For reflection would at once step in and remind him of the motives that pull in other or opposite directions, whereupon he would see to it that no such action ensue. With such a successive presentation of different and mutually exclusive motives, to the constant accompaniment of the inner refrain: "I can do what I will," the will turns at once, like a weathervane on a well-oiled pivot in a changeable wind, to every motive that is presented to it by the imagination. It turns successively to all the motives that lie before it as possible, and with each the human being thinks he can *will* it, and thus fix the weathervane at this point; but this is a mere deception. For his "I can will this" is in truth hypothetical and carries with it the clause "if I did not rather will that other thing"; but this abolishes that ability to will. – Let us turn to the man whom we left deliberating at six o'clock, and imagine that he now notices that I am standing behind him, philosophizing about him, and disputing his

[3] "Wish" or "act of wishing."   [4] "Will" or "act of willing."

freedom to do all those actions that to him are possible. It might easily happen that he carries out one of them in order to refute me; but then my denial of his freedom and its effect on his spirit of contradiction would have been the motive that compelled him to do it. Yet this could induce him to carry out only one or other of the *easier* of the above-listed actions, e.g., to go to the theater, but certainly not the last-mentioned one, namely to run out into the wide world; for such an action, that motive would be much too weak. – In just the same way, many a human being erroneously imagines that, by holding a loaded pistol in his hand, he can shoot himself. The least thing for doing this is the mechanical means of carrying it out, but the main thing is an exceedingly powerful and therefore very rare motive that has the immense strength necessary to overcome the desire for life or rather the fear of death. Only after such a motive has entered can he actually shoot himself, and then he must, unless the deed is prevented by an even stronger countermotive, if such is at all possible.

I can do what I will; I can, *if I will*, give all I have to the poor, and thus become poor myself – if I *will*! – But I am not able to *will* this 44 because the opposing motives have far too much power over me. If, on the other hand, I had another character, indeed to the extent of being a saint, then I could will it; but then I could not help willing it and would therefore have to do it. – All this is perfectly consistent with the "I can *do* what I *will*" of self-consciousness, in which even today some thoughtless philosophasters imagine they see the freedom of the will, and accordingly advance this as a given fact of consciousness. The most conspicuous of these is M. *Cousin*, who therefore merits an honorable mention here, for in his *Cours d'histoire de la philosophie*, given in 1819–20, and published by Vacherot, 1841, he teaches that the freedom of the will is the most reliable fact of consciousness (vol. 1, pp. 19, 20),[5] and censures *Kant* for demonstrating it merely from the moral law and setting it up as a postulate;[6] for, as he says, it is a fact. *"Pourquoi démontrer ce qu'il suffit de constater?"* (p. 50) – *"la liberté est un fait, et non une croyance"* (ibid.).[7] Meanwhile there is no lack of ignorant people even in Germany who disregard all that great thinkers in the

---

[5] Victor Cousin (1792–1867): French philosopher; author of *Course in the History of Philosophy*.
[6] For Kant's deduction of freedom from moral consciousness, see *Critique of Practical Reason*, Academy edition, V, 29–31.
[7] "Why demonstrate what it is sufficient to state? – Freedom is a fact, not a belief."

last two centuries have said on this subject, and who, insisting on the fact of self-consciousness analyzed in the previous section, which they wrongly interpret just like the masses, vaunt the freedom of the will as factually given. Yet perhaps I am doing them an injustice, since it may be that they are not so ignorant as they appear, but are merely hungry, and consequently for a very dry crust of bread teach everything that might be agreeable to some high state ministry.

It is certainly neither metaphor nor hyperbole, but quite sober and literal truth, that a human being can no more get up from his chair before a motive pulls or pushes him than a billiard ball can be set in motion before it is struck; but then his getting up is as necessary and inevitable as is the rolling of the ball after it is struck. And to expect someone to do something without his being urged to do so by any interest at all is like expecting a piece of wood to move toward me without a cord that draws it. If anyone making such an assertion is met with an obstinate contradiction at a gathering, he would be speedily vindicated if he were to get a third person suddenly to call out in a loud and earnest voice: "The beams are collapsing!" In this way the contra-dictors would come to see that for driving people out of the house a motive is just as powerful as the most robust mechanical cause.

For, like all objects of experience, the human being is an appearance in time and space, and as the law of causality is *a priori* valid for all of them and consequently without exception, he also must be subject to it. Thus the pure understanding states it *a priori*; it is confirmed by the analogy that runs through the whole of nature; and it is testified to by experience every moment, unless we are deceived by the illusion created by the fact that the beings of nature become more complex as they rise in the scale, and their susceptibility is enhanced and refined from the merely mechanical to the chemical, electrical, irritable, sensible, intellectual, and finally rational, such that the nature of the *operating causes* must also keep pace with this enhanced susceptibility and at each stage must turn out in conformity with the beings on which they are to operate. Therefore the causes also appear less and less palpable and material, so that at last they are no longer visible to the eye, although still within reach of the understanding, which presup-poses them with unshakable confidence, and also discovers them after a proper search. For here the operating causes are enhanced to mere thoughts that wrestle with other thoughts until the most powerful

45

39

determines the outcome and sets the human being in motion. All this happens with a necessity of causal connection that is just as strict as when purely mechanical causes act against one another in complex conjunction, and the calculated result infallibly enters. On account of the invisibility of the cause, the little electrified cork pellets jumping about in a glass in all directions have the appearance of a lack of causality just as do a human being's movements; but judgment is an affair not of the eye but of the understanding.

46 On the assumption of the freedom of the will, every human action would be an inexplicable miracle – an effect without a cause. If we attempt to represent to our mind such a *liberum arbitrium indifferentiae*, we soon become aware that here the understanding is really brought to a halt; it has no form of thinking such a thing. For the principle of sufficient reason, the principle of the universal determination and dependence of appearances on one another, is the most general form of our faculty of cognition, which itself assumes different shapes according to the differences in the objects of cognition. But in this case we are supposed to think of something that determines without being determined, that depends on nothing, though something else depends on it, that now produces *A* without compulsion and consequently without ground, whereas it could just as well produce *B*, *C*, or *D*, and indeed could do so under the very same circumstances, i.e., without there being in *A* something giving it an advantage over *B*, *C*, or *D* (for this would be motivation and hence causality). Here we are led back to the concept of the *absolutely contingent*, which was presented as problematical at the very beginning of this essay. I repeat that here the understanding is brought to a halt, if we are able to bring it to bear on the problem at all.

But let us now also call to mind what a *cause* in general is, namely an antecedent change rendering necessary the change that follows. No cause in the world produces its effect absolutely and entirely or makes it out of nothing. On the contrary, there is always something on which the cause exercises its efficacy; and the cause merely occasions at this time, in this place, and in this definite being a change which is always in keeping with the nature of the being, and hence the *force* for producing the change had to reside already in that being. Consequently, every effect springs from two factors, an inner and an outer, thus from the original force of the thing acted upon, and from the determining cause compelling that force now to manifest itself here. Every causality and every explanation presupposes some original force; therefore an explanation never explains everything, but always leaves something inexplicable. We see this in the whole of physics and chemistry; in their explanations, the forces of nature are everywhere presupposed; such forces manifest themselves in the phenomena, and the whole explanation consists in reducing things to them. A force of nature itself is not

47 subject to any explanation, but is the principle of all explanation. Nor is a force of nature subject to any causality, but is precisely that which endows every cause with causality, i.e., the capacity to produce an effect. It is itself the common substratum of all the effects of this kind and is present in each of them. Thus the phenomena of magnetism are reduced to an original force called electricity. Here the explanation stops; it gives merely the conditions under which such a force manifests itself, i.e., the causes that call forth its efficacy. The explanations of celestial mechanics presuppose gravitation as the force by virtue of which the particular causes are here effective in determining the course of the heavenly bodies. The explanations of chemistry presuppose the secret forces that manifest themselves as elective affinities according to certain stoichiometric relations. To these forces are ultimately due all the effects which promptly occur when called forth by specified causes. In just the same way, all explanations of physiology presuppose the vital force, which reacts in a definite way to specific inner and outer stimuli. And so it is everywhere. Even the causes dealt with by so comprehensible a science as mechanics, such as impact and pressure, presuppose impenetrability, cohesion, rigidity, hardness, inertia, gravity, elasticity, which are unfathomable forces of nature no less than those just mentioned. Hence causes everywhere determine nothing more than the when and where of the *manifestations* of original, inexplicable forces, and only on their assumption are they causes, i.e., necessarily bring about certain effects.

Now just as this is the case with causes in the narrowest sense and with stimuli, so too is it equally the case with *motives*; for in essence motivation is not different from causality, but is only a form of it, namely causality that passes through the medium of cognition. Therefore here too the cause calls forth only the manifestation of a force that cannot be reduced and consequently cannot be explained any further. The force in question, which is called *will*, is known to us not merely from without as are the other forces of nature, but also from within and immediately by virtue of self-consciousness. Only on the assumption that such a will is present and is of a definite quality in a particular case are the causes directed to it, here called motives, efficacious. This particularly and individually determined quality of the will, by virtue of which the will's reaction to the same motives is different in each human being, constitutes what we call his *character*, and indeed his *empirical character*, since it is known not *a priori* but only through experience. It determines first of all the mode of operation of the different kinds of motives on the given human being. For it underlies all the effects that are called forth by the motives, just as the universal forces of nature underlie the effects that are produced by causes in the narrowest sense, and the vital force underlies the effects of stimuli. Like the forces of nature, this character is also original, unalterable, and inexplicable. In animals it is different in every species; in the human being it is different in every individual. Only in the highest and cleverest of all the animals does there appear a noticeable individual character, although together with the wholly predominant character of the species.

The *character* of a human being is (1) *individual*; it is different in each and every one. It is true that the character of the species underlies them all, and thus the principal qualities are met with again in everyone. But here the variation is so significant, there is such a diversity of combination and modification of qualities by one another, that we can assume the moral difference of characters to be equal to that in intellectual abilities, which is great indeed. And we can further assume that both these differences are incomparably greater than are the bodily differences between giant and dwarf, Apollo and Thersites. Therefore the effect of the same motive on different human beings is quite different, just as sunlight turns wax white but chloride of silver black, and heat softens wax but hardens clay. Therefore from a knowledge of the motive alone, we cannot predict the deed, but for this the character must also be precisely known.

(2) The character of a human being is *empirical*. Only through experience do we come to know it, not merely in others but also in ourselves. This is why we are often disillusioned, with regard to ourselves and to others alike, when we discover that we do not possess this or that quality, e.g., justice, unselfishness, courage, in the degree we fondly assumed. Therefore in a difficult choice before us our own

resolve, like that of another, remains a secret to us until the choice is decided. We believe the choice will fall now on one side, now on the other, according as this or that motive is held nearer to the will by cognition and tries its strength on it. Here the "I can do what I will" produces the illusion of freedom of the will. Finally, the stronger motive asserts its power over the will, and the choice often proves to be different from what we at first imagined. In the end, therefore, no one can know how either someone else or he himself will act in some definite situation until that human being has been in it. Only after the test has been made is he certain of the other person and only then of himself as well. But then he is certain; tried friends, tested servants are safe. In general we treat a human being whom we thoroughly know as we treat everything else whose properties we have come to know; and we foresee with confidence what may or may not be expected of him. Whoever has done something once will do it again, whether for good or for evil, when the opportunity presents itself. And so a human being who needs great and extraordinary help will turn to one who has shown proofs of generosity; and if he wants to hire an assassin, he will look for one among those who have already steeped their hands in blood. According to Herodotus[8] (*Historiai*, VII, 164), Gelon of Syracuse was under the necessity of entrusting a very large sum of money entirely to one man, for he had to give it to him to take abroad, and it was wholly at the man's disposal. For this work he chose Cadmus, who had given proof of rare and even unheard-of integrity and conscientiousness. His trust was perfectly justified. – Similarly only from experience and when the opportunity comes does there arise an acquaintance with ourselves on which rests a confidence or distrust in our nature. Accordingly, as we have shown in a given case reflectiveness, courage, integrity, reticence, refinement, or whatever else the case might have required, or if a lack of such virtues has come to light, we are afterward satisfied or dissatisfied with ourselves in consequence of the acquaintance we have made of our own nature. Only a precise knowledge of his own empirical character gives a human being what is called an *acquired character*. It is possessed by the human being who knows precisely his own qualities, both good and bad, and thus knows for certain what he may and may not count on and expect from himself. He now plays skillfully and

50

---

[8] Herodotus (ca. 480–ca. 420 B.C.): Greek historian, the "father of history" (Cicero). Author of *Historiai* (*Histories*).

methodically, with firmness and dignity, his own part, which he formerly played only by the light of nature in virtue of his empirical character. He now plays it without ever, as we say, acting out of his character, which latter always shows that in a particular case a man was mistaken about himself.

(3) The character of a human being is *constant*; it remains the same throughout his whole life. Under the changeable mask of his years, his circumstances, and even his cognitions and views, we find the real identical human being, like a crab in its shell, quite unchangeable and always the same. Merely in direction and material does his character undergo the apparent modifications that are a consequence of the difference in the stages of his life and their needs. *A human being never changes*; as he has acted in a given case, so will he always act again in exactly the same circumstances (to which, however, also belongs a correct knowledge of those circumstances). We can obtain confirmation of this truth from daily experience; but the most striking is obtained when after twenty or thirty years we meet an acquaintance again and soon spot in him precisely the same old tricks as before. – Many a human being, of course, will deny this truth in words; yet he himself presupposes it in his actions, for he never again trusts anyone whom he has *once* found to be dishonest, whereas he relies on the one who has previously shown himself to be honest. For the possibility of all our knowledge of human beings and of our firm trust of those who have been proven, tried, and confirmed rests on this truth. Even when such a confidence has once deceived us, we never say "His character has changed," but "I was mistaken about him." – It is owing to this truth that, when we wish to estimate the moral worth of an action, we first try to reach certainty as to its motive; yet our praise or blame is later directed not to the motive, but to the character that allowed itself to be determined thereby, which is the second factor of this deed and the only one inherent in the human being. – It depends on the same truth that true honor (not knightly honor, which is fool's honor) once lost can never be restored; the stain of a single unworthy action sticks to the human being forever. Hence the proverb: "Once a thief, always a thief." – Again, in important political affairs, it may be desirable to resort to treason, and therefore a traitor is sought, made use of, and rewarded. But when the object is attained, prudence demands his removal, because the circumstances can change, but not his character. –

51

Again, the greatest failing in a dramtic poet is for his characters not to be fixed, i.e., for them not to be carried through, like those depicted by the great poets, with the constancy and strict consistency of a natural force. In the *Parerga*, vol. II, § 118, p. 196 of the first edition, I have demonstrated this in a detailed example from Shakespeare. – Indeed, on the same truth depends the possibility of conscience, insofar as the latter often holds before us late in life the misdeeds of our youth, as, for example, in the case of J.-J. Rousseau[9] forty years after he had accused the servant girl Marion of a theft he himself had committed. This is possible only on the assumption that the character has remained the same and unchanged; on the other hand, we are not ashamed in old age of the most ridiculous errors, the greatest ignorance, or the strangest follies of our youth. For all these were matters of cognition and have changed; we have given them up and long since laid them aside, as we did the clothes of our youth. – It is owing to the same truth that, even in spite of the clearest knowledge, even detestation, of his moral failings and shortcomings, in spite of the sincerest intention to reform, a human being nevertheless does not really change for the better, but notwithstanding the most serious resolutions and sincere promises, allows himself, to his own astonishment, to pursue the same old paths again when the opportunity is renewed. Only his *cognition* can be corrected; thus he may come to see that the particular means formerly employed by him do not lead to the end he has in view, or that they entail more disadvantage than gain; he then changes the means but not the ends. The American penitential system is based on this point; it does not undertake to reform a human being's *character* or *heart*, but to put his *head* right and show him that it will be for him far more difficult, much more troublesome and dangerous, to attain the ends to which he immutably aspires by virtue of his character on the path of dishonesty, hitherto pursued by him, than on that of honesty, work, and contentment. In general the sphere and domain of all correction and improvement lie in *cognition* alone. The character is unalterable; the motives operate with necessity, but they have to pass through *cognition*, the medium of the motives. Cognition, however, is capable of the most manifold extension, of constant correction in innumerable degrees; all

52

---

[9] Jean-Jacques Rousseau (1712–78): French-Swiss philosopher, novelist, botanist, and man of letters. The wrongful accusation of the maid is related in his autobiography, *Les confessions* (*Confessions*), published in 1781–88.

education works to this end. Cultivation of reason by cognitions and insights of every kind is morally important, because it opens the way to motives which would be closed off to the human being without it. As long as he was unable to understand them, they were nonexistent for his will. Thus in identical external circumstances, a human being's position can in fact be quite different the second time from what it was the first, if in the meantime he has been able correctly and fully to understand those circumstances. In this way, motives by which he was previously unaffected now have an effect on him. In this sense the scholastic philosophers were quite right in saying: *causa finalis* (purpose, motive) *movet non secundum suum esse reale, sed secundum esse cognitum.*[10] But no moral influence goes beyond the correction of cognition; and to undertake to eliminate a human being's defects of character by lecturing and moralizing, and thus to seek to reform his character itself, his actual morality, is like trying through external influence to turn lead into gold, or by careful cultivation to make an oak bear apricots.

53   We find the conviction of the unalterable nature of character expressed unequivocally already by *Apuleius* in his *Oratio de magia.*[11] Defending himself against the charge of sorcery, he appeals in this work to his well-known character, and says: *Certum indicem cujusque animum esse, qui semper eodem ingenio ad virtutem vel ad malitiam moratus, firmum argumentum est accipiendi criminis, aut respuendi.*[12]

(4) The individual character is *inborn*; it is not a work of art or circumstances subject to chance, but that of nature herself. It reveals itself even in the child, there showing on a small scale what in the future it will be on a large. Hence, in spite of the greatest similarity of upbringing and environment, two children evince most clearly an extreme difference of character; it is the same character that they will bear when they are advanced in years. In its basic features character is even hereditary, but only from the father; intelligence, on the other hand, comes from the mother. On this point I refer to chapter 43 of the second volume of my main work.

---

[10] "The final cause operates not according to its real being, but to how it is cognized."

[11] Apuleius (ca. 123): rhetorician and priest. The exact title of the work to which Schopenhauer refers is *Apologia* or *Pro se de Magia* (*Apology* or *Self-Defense Concerning Magic*).

[12] "A sure proof is to be found in the character of every human being, which by nature is always disposed in the same way to virtue or malice and is a solid ground for committing a crime or refraining from it."

From this explanation of the essence of the individual character, it certainly follows that virtues and vices are inborn. This truth may be inconvenient to many a prejudice and to many a system of spinning-wheel philosophy with its so-called practical interests, i.e., with its petty narrow conceptions and limited grade-school views. Yet it was already the conviction of *Socrates*, the father of morals, who according to Aristotle's statement (*Magna moralia*, I, 9, 1187a 7) maintained: οὐκ ἐφ' ἡμῖν γενέσθαι τὸ σπουδαίους εἶναι, ἢ φαύλους (*in arbitrio nostro positum non esse, nos probos, vel malos esse*).[13] What Aristotle says there against this is obviously worthless; he himself also shares that opinion of Socrates and expresses it most clearly in the *Nicomachean Ethics*, VI, 13, 1144b 4, where he says: Πᾶσι γὰρ δοκεῖ ἕκαστα τῶν ἠθῶν ὑπάρχειν φύσει πως· καὶ γὰρ δίκαιοι καὶ σωφρονικοὶ καὶ ἀνδρεῖοι καὶ τἄλλα ἔχομεν εὐθὺς ἐκ γενετῆς (*Singuli enim mores in omnibus hominibus quodammodo videntur inesse natura: namque ad justitiam, temperantiam, fortitudinem, ceterasque virtutes proclivitatem statim habemus, cum primum nascimur*).[14] And if we survey all the virtues and vices in Aristotle's work, *On Virtues and Vices*, where they are brought together in a short résumé, we shall find that all of them in actual human beings can only be conceived as *inborn* qualities, and only as such would they be genuine. Arising from reflection, on the other hand, and arbitrarily assumed, they would really amount to a kind of *dissimulation* and would be ungenuine; and so it would be absolutely impossible to count on their continued existence and confirmation under stressful circumstances. And if we add the Christian virtue of love, *caritas*, unknown to Aristotle and all the ancients, it is no different in this regard. How could the inexhaustible goodness of one human being and the incorrigible, deep-rooted wickedness of another, the character of the Antonines, of Hadrian and Titus, on the one hand, and that of Caligula, Nero, and Domitian, on the other,[15] have come suddenly from without and be the work of chance circumstances or of

---

[13] "That it is not in our power to be good or bad."

[14] "For, as it seems, the particular traits of character are already in some way by nature peculiar to all; for a tendency to justice, moderation, bravery, and the like is already peculiar to us from birth."

[15] The Antonines were the Roman emperors Antoninus Pius (86–161) and Marcus Aurelius Antoninus (121–80). The other Roman emperors mentioned by Schopenhauer are Publius Aelius Hadrianus (76–138), Titus Flavius Vespasianus (9–79), Caius Julius Caesar Germanicus, called Caligula (baby boots) (12–41), Nero Claudius Caesar (37–68) and Titus Flavius Domitianus (51–96).

mere cognition and instruction! Indeed, it was Nero who had Seneca[16] as a tutor. – On the contrary, the seed of all the virtues and vices of a human being lies in the inborn character, in that real kernel of the whole human being. This conviction, which is natural to one who is unprejudiced, guided the hand of *Velleius Paterculus*[17] when he wrote the following about Cato[18] (*Historiae romanae*, II, 35, 2): *Homo virtuti consimillimus, et per omnia genio diis, quam hominibus propior: qui nunquam recte fecit, ut facere videretur, sed quia ALITER FACERE NON POTERAT.*[19] [d]

On the other hand, if we assume the freedom of the will, it is absolutely impossible to see how virtue and vice are really supposed to originate, or in general to explain the fact that two human beings, brought up in an identical manner, act quite differently, and even do opposite things, in precisely the same circumstances and on the

55   same occasions. The actual, original, and fundamental difference of characters is irreconcilable with the assumption of a freedom of the will which consists in saying that, for any human in any situation, opposite actions are supposed to be equally possible. For then his character must be from the very beginning a *tabula rasa*,[20] like the intellect according to *Locke*,[21] and cannot have any inborn inclination to one side or the other, since the latter would suspend already the perfect equilibrium

---

[16] Lucius Annaeus Seneca (between 4 B.C. and A.D. I to A.D. 65): Roman orator, statesman, poet, and philosopher.

[17] Velleius Paterculus (b. 20 B.C.): Roman historian. Author of *Roman History.*

[18] Marcus Porcius Cato (95–46 B.C.): Roman aristocrat, politician, and Stoic.

[19] "A man who was most closely akin to virtue and was in all respects by his natural disposition nearer to the gods than to humans; a man who never did right for the sake of appearances, but because *he could not act otherwise.*"

[20] "Blank slate."

[21] See *An Essay Concerning Human Understanding*, bk. II, chap. I, sect. 2, where Locke characterizes the original state of the mind as that of a "white paper."

[d] This passage is gradually becoming a regular weapon in the armory of the determinists. The good old historian of eighteen centuries ago certainly never dreamt of such an honor. *Hobbes* first commended it, and after him *Priestley*. Then *Schelling* reproduced it in his treatise on freedom, p. 478, in a translation that was somewhat tampered with to suit his own ends. Therefore he does not mention Velleius Paterculus by name, but says, with shrewdness as well as with superior airs, "one of the ancients." Finally, I, too, did not want to omit to quote it, for it is really to the point. [In addition to mentioning the English philosopher, political theorist, and scientist Thomas Hobbes (1588–1679) and the English scientist, minister, theologian, and philosopher Joseph Priestley (1733–1804), whose positions on the freedom of the will are presented in section four of the *Prize Essay*, Schopenhauer here refers to a work by the German philosopher Friedrich Wilhelm Joseph Schelling (1775–1854) entitled *Philosophical Inquiries into the Essence of Human Freedom*, published in 1809].

that one thinks of in the *liberum arbitrium indifferentiae*. Thus on the assumption of such a freedom of the will, the reason why different human beings act in different ways as we have been considering, cannot be found in the *subjective*. But still less in the *objective*; for then it would indeed be the objects that determined the acting, and the required freedom would be lost entirely. There might possibly be left a way out, namely to put midway between subject and object the origin of that actual great diversity in the ways of acting, and thus to have it originate from the different manner in which the objective would be apprehended by the subjective, i.e., the manner in which it would be *known* by different persons. But then everything would be reduced to correct or incorrect *cognition* of the circumstances of the moment. Thus the moral difference between the ways of acting would be transformed into a mere difference in the correctness of judgment, and morals would be turned into logic. Now the advocates of freedom of the will might attempt finally to rescue themselves from that grievous dilemma by saying that there is, of course, no inborn difference of characters, but that such difference would arise from external circumstances, impressions, experiences, example, teachings, and so on. They might say that, once the character is established in this way, the diversity of action can be subsequently explained from it. The answer to this is first that the character would accordingly put in a very late appearance (whereas, as a matter of fact, it can be recognized already in children), and most people would die before having acquired a character; but secondly, that all those external circumstances whose work is said to be the formation of the character lie entirely outside our power, and are produced in some way or other by chance (or Providence if the term be preferred). Therefore if from these circumstances the character arose, and from the latter in turn the diversity of action, then all moral responsibility for that diversity would completely and entirely disappear, for ultimately it would obviously be the work of chance or Providence. Therefore, on the assumption of freedom of the will, we see the origin of the different ways of acting and thus of virtue or vice, together with responsibility, floating about without any support and nowhere finding a small corner in which to take root. But it follows from this that, however much it may appeal at first sight to the untutored understanding, yet at bottom that assumption still stands just as much in contradiction to our moral convictions as to the primary fundamental rule of our understanding, as I have sufficiently shown.

56

The necessity with which, as I have previously demonstrated in some detail, motives operate, like all causes in general, is not one without presupposition. We have now come to know its presupposition, or the ground on which it rests; it is the inborn, *individual character*. Just as every effect in inanimate nature is a necessary product of two factors, namely the universal *natural force* here manifesting itself and the particular *cause* here calling forth that manifestation, so in the same way is every deed of a human being the necessary product of his *character* and the *motive* that has entered. If these two are given, the deed inevitably ensues. For a different deed to arise, either a different motive or a different character would have to be posited. Moreover, every deed could be predicted, in fact calculated, with certainty, if it were not for the fact that the character is very difficult to fathom, and also that the motive is often concealed and always exposed to the contrary effect of other motives, which lie solely in the sphere of thoughts of the human being and are inaccessible to others. The ends in general to which a human being invariably aspires are already essentially determined by his inborn character. The means to these ends to which he resorts are determined partly by the external circumstances and partly by his comprehension of them, whose correctness in turn depends on his understanding and its formation. Now as the final result of all this, his individual deeds ensue and consequently the entire role he has to play 57 in the world. We find expressed in one of Goethe's[22] finest stanzas, with equal accuracy and poetry, the result of the doctrine concerning individual character which I have discussed here:

> "As on the day that lent you to the world
> The sun received the planets' greetings,
> At once and eternally you have thrived
> According to the law whereby you stepped forth.
> So must you be, from yourself you cannot flee,
> So have the Sibyls and the Prophets said;
> No time, no power breaks into little pieces
> The form here stamped and in life developed."[23]

Therefore that presupposition on which the necessity of the effects of all causes in general rests is the inner essence of each and every thing, whether the latter be merely a universal natural force manifesting itself

[22] Johann Wolfgang von Goethe (1749–1832): German poet, statesman, and scientist.
[23] "Dämon" ("Demon"), from *Urworte. Orphisch* (*Orphic Primal Words*), first published in 1820.

in it, or vital force, or will. Every being, of whatever kind, will always react in accordance with its peculiar nature to the occasion of the influencing causes. This law, to which everything in the world is subject without exception, was expressed by the scholastic philosophers in the formula *operari sequitur esse*.[24] In consequence of it, the chemist tests bodies by reagents, and a human being tests a human being by experiments to which he subjects him. In all cases the external causes will necessarily call forth that which is found in the being; for the latter cannot react in any other way than in the one in which it exists.

Here we must remember that every *existentia* presupposes an *essentia*; that is to say, everything that is must also be *something*, must have a definite essence. It cannot *exist* and yet at the same time be *nothing*, thus something like the *ens metaphysicum*,[25] i.e., something that *is* and only *is*, without any determinations and qualities, and consequently without the definite mode of action that flows from these. Just as an *essentia* without *existentia* furnishes no reality (Kant illustrated this by the well-known example of the hundred thalers),[26] in the same way an *existentia* without *essentia* is unable to furnish a reality. For everything that is must have a nature essential and peculiar to it, by virtue of which it is what it is, which it always maintains and the manifestations of which are called forth by causes with necessity; whereas this nature itself is by no means the work of those causes, nor can it be modified through them. But all this is just as true of the human being and his will as of all the other beings in nature. He too has an *essentia* in addition to an *existentia*, i.e., he has fundamental essential qualities that constitute his very character and require only occasioning from without in order to come forth. Consequently, to expect a human being on the same occasion to act at one time in one way and at another in an entirely different way would be like expecting the same tree which bears cherries this summer to bear pears the next. Closely considered, the freedom of the will means an *existentia* without *essentia*; this is equivalent to saying that something *is* and yet at the same time *is nothing*, which again means that it *is not* and thus is a contradiction.

We must attribute to insight into that truth as well as into the *a priori* certain and hence exceptionless validity of the law of causality the fact

---

[24] "Doing follows being."   [25] "Metaphysical being."

[26] See *Critique of Pure Reason*, A 599/B 627, where Kant argues that a hundred actual thalers do not contain the least bit more than a hundred possible ones.

that all really profound thinkers of all times, however different their other views, have agreed in maintaining the necessity of the acts of will upon entering motives and in rejecting the *liberum arbitrium*. Since the immense majority of those who are incapable of thinking and are exposed to delusion and prejudice have always obstinately opposed this truth, those thinkers have even taken it to extremes in order to assert it in the most decided and indeed exuberant terms. The best-known of these is *Buridan's* ass,[27] yet during the last hundred years a search for it has been made in vain in the writings of Buridan that still exist. I myself possess a copy of his *Sophismata*, printed apparently already in the fifteenth century, yet without place of origin, year, or page numbering. In it I have often searched in vain for this, although on almost every page asses occur as examples. *Bayle*,[28] whose article on *Buridan* is the basis of all that has since been written on the subject, says quite wrongly that we know of only the one *sophisma* of Buridan, for I have a whole quarto volume of *sophismata* by him. Because *Bayle* deals with the subject at such length, he also ought to have known what seems to have escaped notice since then as well, namely that that example, which has become to some extent the symbol or type of the great truth I am upholding, is far older than *Buridan*. It is found in *Dante*,[29] who was master of all the learning of his age and lived before Buridan. In the following words, with which the fourth book of his *Paradiso* opens, he speaks not of asses but of human beings:

> *Intra duo cibi, distanti e moventi*
> *D'un modo, prima si morrìa di fame,*
> *Che liber' uomo l'un recasse a' denti.*[e]

In fact we even find it in Aristotle, *On the Heavens*, II, 13, 295b 32, where he says: καὶ ὁ λόγος τοῦ πεινῶντος καὶ διψῶντος σφόδρα μέν, ὁμοίως δὲ, καὶ τῶν ἐδωδίμων καί ποτῶν ἴσον ἀπέχοντος, καὶ

---

[27] John Buridan (ca. 1295/1300–1360): Christian theologian and philosopher. His *Sophismata* (*Sophisms*) was first printed in 1489.

[28] Pierre Bayle (1647–1706): French man of letters. His *Dictionnaire historique et critique* (*Historical and Critical Dictionary*), published in 1695–97, contains an entry on Buridan.

[29] Dante Alighieri (1265–1321): Florentine statesman, political theorist, and poet. The *Paradiso* (*Paradise*) is the third and final book of *La Divina Commedia* (*The Divine Comedy*).

[e] *Inter duos cibos aeque remotos unoque modo motos constitutus, homo prius fame periret, quam ut, absoluta libertate usus, unum eorum dentibus admoveret.* ["Placed between two kinds of food equidistant and uniformly moved, a man would die of hunger before he of his own free will brought one of them to his mouth."]

γὰρ τοῦτον ἠρεμεῖν ἀναγκαῖον (*item ea, quae de sitiente vehementer esurienteque dicuntur, cum aeque ab his, quae eduntur atque bibuntur, distat: quiescat enim necesse est*).[30] Buridan, who had obtained the example from these sources, substituted an ass for the human being merely because it was the custom of this poor scholastic to take for his examples either Socrates and Plato or *asinus*.

The question concerning the freedom of the will is really a touchstone whereby we can distinguish the deep-thinking minds from the superficial ones, or a boundary stone where the two part company, since the former all assert the necessary ensuing of the action when the character and motive are given, whereas the latter with the crowd cling to freedom of the will. Then there is yet an intermediate party which, feeling perplexed, tacks here and there, shifts the target point for itself and others, takes refuge behind words and phrases, or so twists and turns the question until we no longer know what it was about. This was done already by *Leibniz*, who was much more a mathematician and polyhistor than a philosopher.[f] But to bring such talkers to the point, we must put the question to them in the following form and must stand by it:

(1) For a given human being in given circumstances, are two actions possible, or is only *one*? The answer of all deep thinkers is: only one.

(2) Supposing that a given human being's character remained unalterable on the one hand, and, on the other, the circumstances whose influence he had to undergo were necessarily determined thoroughly and down to the smallest detail by external causes, which always enter with strict necessity, and whose chain, consisting entirely of links just as necessary, runs back to infinity – supposing all this, could the past course of such a human being's life turn out, even in the smallest particular, in any event or scene, differently from the way in which it did? – No is the consistent and correct answer.

The conclusion from these two propositions is that *everything that happens, from the greatest to the smallest, happens necessarily. Quidquid fit, necessario fit.*

Whoever is shocked by these propositions has something still to learn

---

[30] "Likewise the example of the human being suffering from hunger and thirst in an equally high degree, if he is equally remote from food and drink: he too must of necessity remain immobile."

[f] Leibniz's inconsistency on this point is most clearly shown in his letter to Coste of 19 December 1707, *Opera philosophica*, ed. Erdmann, p. 447, and then in the *Théodicée*, §§ 45–53.

and something else to unlearn; but then he will recognize that they are the most fruitful source of consolation and peace of mind. – Our deeds are certainly not a first beginning, so that in them nothing really new comes into existence, but *by what we do we merely come to know what we are.*

Even if not clearly recognized, the conviction of the strict necessity of all that happens is at any rate felt, as in the view of *fatum*, εἱμαρμένη,[31] that was so firmly held by the ancients, and in the fatalism of the Mohammedans, even in the universal and ineradicable belief in *omina*.[32] This is simply because even the smallest accident occurs necessarily, and all events, so to speak, keep time with one another, and so everything resonates in everything else. Finally, closely connected with this is the fact that whoever has wounded or killed another quite unintentionally and accidentally is afflicted all his life by this *piaculum*[33] with a feeling that seems to be akin to that of guilt, and also experiences a peculiar kind of discredit by others as a *persona piacularis* (a person of evil omen). Indeed, the felt conviction of the unalterability of character and of the necessity of its manifestations has not been without influence even on the Christian doctrine of predestination. – Finally, I will not refrain from making here the following entirely incidental remark, which anyone, according as he reflects on certain things, may accept or drop as he thinks fit. If we do not accept the strict necessity of all that happens by virtue of a causal chain that connects all events without distinction, but represent that chain as being interrupted in innumerable places by an absolute freedom, then all *foreseeing of the future* in dreams, in clairvoyant somnambulism, and in second sight becomes even *objectively*, and thus absolutely, *impossible* and consequently inconceivable. For then there is absolutely no objectively real future that could possibly be foreseen. By contrast, we are now in doubt only about the *subjective* conditions for foreseeing the future and hence about the *subjective* possibility. And at the present time even this doubt can no longer be entertained by those who are well informed, after innumerable testimonies of the greatest veracity have established those anticipations of the future.

I add a few more remarks as corollaries to the established doctrine of the necessity of all that happens.

[31] "Fate."   [32] Plural of "omen" or "sign."   [32] "An act which demands expiation."

What would become of this world if necessity did not permeate all things and hold them together, but especially if it did not preside over the generation of individuals? A monster, a rubbish heap, a caricature without sense and significance – the work of true and utter chance. –

To wish that some event had not happened is a foolish piece of self-torture, for it is equivalent to wishing something absolutely impossible; it is as irrational as to wish that the sun would rise in the west. Just because all that happens, both great and small, occurs with *strict* necessity, it is quite futile to reflect on it and to think how trifling and fortuitous were the causes that led to that event, and how very easily they could have been other than they were. For this is an illusion, since they have all occurred with just as strict a necessity and have operated with a force just as perfect as that in consequence of which the sun rises in the east. On the contrary, we should regard the events as they occur with just the same eye with which we read the printed word, well knowing that it was there before we read it.

62

IV
Predecessors

In support of the previous statement about the judgment of all deep thinkers with regard to our problem, I will call to mind some of the great men who have expressed themselves in this sense.

First, to reassure those who might possibly think that religious grounds are opposed to the truth I advocate, I recall what Jeremiah (x, 23) has said: "The way of man is not in himself; it is not in man that walketh to direct his steps." But in particular I refer to *Luther*, who in a book specially written on this subject, *De servo arbitrio*,[1] contests with all his vehemence the freedom of the will. A few passages from it will suffice to show the character of his opinion; naturally he supports the latter not with philosophical but with theological reasons. I quote from the edition of Seb. Schmidt, Strasburg, 1707. – On page 145 it says: *Quare simul in omnium cordibus scriptum invenitur liberum arbitrium nihil esse; licet obscuretur tot disputationibus contrariis et tanta tot virorum auctoritate. – P.* 214: *Hoc loco admonitos velim liberi arbitrii tutores, ut sciant, sese esse abnegatores Christi, dum asserunt liberum arbitrium. – P.* 220: *Contra liberum arbitrium pugnabunt Scripturae testimonia, quot-* 64 *quot de Christo loquuntur. At ea sunt innumerabilia, imo tota Scriptura. Ideo, si Scriptura judice causam agimus, omnibus modis vicero, ut ne jota unum aut apex sit reliquus, qui non damnet dogma liberi arbitrii.*[2]

---

[1] Martin Luther (1483–1546): German theologian and leader of the Protestant Reformation. *De servo arbitrio* (*On the Bondage of the Will*) was published in 1525.

[2] "Therefore we find it equally inscribed in the hearts of all that there is no such thing as free will, although this conviction is obscured by so many assertions to the contrary and by manifold authorities. – Here I would like to remind the advocates of the freedom of the will that, with such freedom, they are deniers of Christ. – The freedom of the will is opposed by all the evidence (of Scripture) which deals with Christ. But such passages are innumerable, since the whole of Scripture deals with him. If, therefore, we plead our cause before the bar of Scripture, I

We now turn to the philosophers. Here the ancients cannot be seriously considered, for their philosophy, still in a state of innocence, so to speak, had not yet become clearly aware of the two most profound and thorny problems of modern philosophy, the question of the freedom of the will and that of the reality of the external world, or about the relation of the ideal to the real. From Aristotle's *Nicomachean Ethics*, III, c. 1–8, we can see pretty well to what extent the problem of the freedom of the will had become clear to the ancients. In that work we find that his thinking on the matter deals essentially with physical and intellectual freedom, and thus he always speaks only of ἑκούσιον καὶ ἀκούσιον,[3] taking voluntary and free as identical. The much more difficult problem of *moral freedom* has not yet presented itself to him, although at times his thoughts certainly do extend that far, especially in *Nicomachean Ethics*, II, 2, and III, 7; but here he falls into the error of deriving character from deeds instead of vice versa. He also quite wrongly criticized the conviction of Socrates, already quoted by me. But in other passages he again adopted the latter as his own, e.g., *Nicomachean Ethics*, x, 9, 1179b 21: τὸ μὲν οὖν τῆς φύσεως δῆλον ὡς οὐκ ἐφ᾽ ἡμῖν ὑπάρχει, ἀλλὰ διά τινας θείας αἰτίας τοῖς ὡς ἀληθῶς εὐτυχέσιν ὑπάρχει (*quod igitur a natura tribuitur, id in nostra potestate non esse, sed, ab aliqua divina causa profectum, inesse in iis, qui revera sunt fortunati, perspicuum est*).[4] – 1179b 29: Δεῖ δὴ τὸ ἦθος προϋπάρχειν πως οἰκεῖον τῆς ἀρετῆς, στέργον τὸ καλὸν καὶ δυσχεραῖνον τὸ αἰσχρόν (*Mores igitur ante quodammodo insint oportet, ad virtutem accommodati, qui honestum amplectantur, turpitudineque offendantur*);[5] this agrees with the passage previously quoted by me and also with *Magna moralia*, I, 11, 1187b 28: Οὐκ ἔσται ὁ προαιρούμενος εἶναι σπουδαιότατος, ἂν μὴ καὶ ἡ φύσις ὑπάρξῃ, βελτίων μέντοι ἔσται (*non enim ut quisque voluerit, erit omnium optimus, nisi etiam natura exstiterit: melior quidem recte erit*).[6] Aristotle deals with the question 65 concerning the freedom of the will in the same sense in the *Magna*

---

shall triumph in every way, since not a jot or tittle is left which does not condemn the doctrine of free will."
[3] "Voluntary and involuntary."
[4] "But as regards the natural disposition, it is clear that this does not lie in our power, but belongs to the truly fortunate by virtue of divine dispensation."
[5] "Therefore, in some way, there must exist beforehand that character which is akin to virtue – loving what is noble, and hating what is bad."
[6] "One cannot become the best by mere intention, unless there also exists the natural disposition so to become; but yet one will become better."

moralia, I, 9–18, and the *Eudemian Ethics*, II, 6–10, where he comes somewhat nearer to the real problem; yet everything is vague and superficial. It is always his method not to go directly into things by treating them analytically, but to draw conclusions synthetically from external marks. Instead of penetrating to the very core of things, he keeps to external signs and even words. This method easily leads us astray, and in the deeper problems never takes us to the goal. Here he stops before the supposed antithesis between the necessary and the voluntary, ἀναγκαῖον καὶ ἑκούσιον, as before a wall. Beyond this, however, there lies the insight that the voluntary *is* precisely *necessary as such*, by virtue of the motive without which an act of will is just as impossible as it is without a subject that wills. For a motive is just as much a cause as is a mechanical cause, from which it differs only in the inessential. Aristotle himself says *(Eudemian Ethics*, II, 10, 1226b 26): ἡ γὰρ οὗ ἕνεκα μία τῶν αἰτίων ἐστίν (*nam id, cujus gratia, una e causarum numero est*).[7] Therefore that antithesis between the voluntary and the necessary is fundamentally false, although even today it is just the same with many alleged philosophers as it was with Aristotle.

Cicero presents the problem of the freedom of the will fairly clearly in the work *De fato*, c. 10 and c. 17.[8] The subject of his treatise, of course, leads to it very easily and naturally. He himself adheres to the freedom of the will, but we see that already Chrysippus[9] and Diodorus[10] must have become more or less clearly aware of the problem. – Also worthy of note is the thirtieth of *Lucian's Dialogues of the Dead*,[11] between Minos and Sostratos, which denies the freedom of the will and with it responsibility.

To a certain extent the fourth book of the Maccabees in the *Septuagint*[12] (which is missing in Luther)[13] is a treatise on the freedom of the will insofar as it sets itself the task of proving that reason (λογισμός) possesses the power to overcome all passions and affects,

---

[7] "For purpose is one of the kinds of causes."
[8] Marcus Tullius Cicero (106–43 B.C.): Roman orator, statesman, writer, and philosopher. Author of *De fato* (*On Fate*).
[9] Chrysippus (ca. 280–207 B.C.): philosopher and third head of the Stoic school.
[10] Diodorus Cronus of Iasos (ca. 300 B.C.): Greek philosopher of the Megarian school of dialectics.
[11] Lucian (ca. A.D. 120): Greek orator and writer. Author of *Nekrikoi dialogoi* (*Dialogues of the Dead*).
[12] Chief Greek version of the Old Testament. Composed after 250 B.C.
[13] In Luther's translation of the Bible into German.

and supports this by the account of the Jewish martyrs in the second book.

66   The oldest author known to me who clearly recognizes our problem appears to be *Clement of Alexandria*,[14] in that he says (*Stromata*, I, c. 17, § 83): οὔτε δὲ οἱ ἔπαινοι, οὔτε οἱ ψόγοι, οὔθ᾽ αἱ τιμαί, οὔθ᾽ αἱ κολάσεις, δίκαιαι, μὴ τῆς ψυχῆς ἐχούσης τὴν ἐξουσίαν τῆς ὁρμῆς καὶ ἀφορμῆς, ἀλλ᾽ ἀκουσίου τῆς κακίας οὔσης (*nec laudes, nec vituperationes, nec honores, nec supplicia justa sunt, si anima non habeat liberam potestatem et appetendi et abstinendi, sed sit vitium involuntarium*).[15] – Then, after a sentence referring to something said previously, he says: ἵν᾽ ὅτι μάλιστα ὁ θεὸς μὲν ἡμῖν κακίας ἀναίτιος (*ut vel maxime quidem Deus nobis non sit causa vitii*).[16] This very remarkable conclusion shows in what sense the Church at once grasped the problem, and what decision she immediately anticipated in accordance with her interests. – Nearly two hundred years later we find the doctrine of free will fully dealt with by *Nemesius*[17] in his work *De natura hominis*, at the end of chap. 35, and in chaps. 39–41. Here the freedom of the will is identified simply with voluntary choice or elective decision, and is accordingly most fervently maintained and substantiated. However, it is already an examination of the subject.

But we find a fully developed awareness of our problem, with all that adheres to it, first in *Augustine*, the Church Father. Therefore, although he is much more a theologian than a philosopher, he is to be considered here. Yet we see at once how the problem puts him into an evident quandary and uncertain hesitation; it leads him into inconsistencies and contradictions in his three books *De libero arbitrio*. On the one hand, he will not, like *Pelagius*,[18] concede to the freedom of the will so much as to abolish original sin, the necessity for salvation, and free predestination, so that the human being could become righteous and worthy of eternal bliss by his own strength. In the part on *De libero arbitrio* from

---

[14] Clement of Alexandria (Titus Flavius Clemens) (ca. 150–ca. 215): Christian theologian and philosopher of Greek descent. Author of eight books of *Stromateis* (Latin *Stromata; Miscellany*), written probably ca. 200–2.

[15] "Neither praise nor blame, neither honor nor reprimand are justified if the soul does not possess the power of striving and resistance, but wickedness is involuntary."

[16] "So that God is above all not to blame for our wickedness."

[17] Nemesius (ca. 400): philosopher and Bishop of Emesa in Syria. Author of *De natura hominis* (*On Human Nature*).

[18] Pelagius (ca. 360–431): Christian heretic who devalued the importance of divine grace for the achievement of salvation. His teachings constitute Pelagianism.

his *Retractationes*,[19] lib. I, c. 9, he even gives one to understand that he would have said still more for this side of the controversy (later so vehemently championed by Luther) if those books had not been written before the appearance of *Pelagius*, against whose opinion he then wrote the book *De natura et gratia*.[20] However, he says already in *De libero arbitrio*, III, 18, § 51: *Nunc autem homo non est bonus, nec habet in potestate, ut bonus sit, sive non videndo qualis esse debeat, sive videndo et non volendo esse, qualem debere esse se videt.*[21] – A bit later: *vel ignorando non habet liberum arbitrium voluntatis ad eligendum quid recte faciat; vel resitente carnali consuetudine, quae violentia mortalis successionis quodam-modo naturaliter inolevit, videat quid recte faciendum sit et velit, nec possit implere;*[22] and in the above-mentioned *Retractationes*, lib. I, c. 9, § 4, he says: *Voluntas ergo ipsa, nisi gratia Dei liberatur a servitute, qua facta est serva peccati, et, ut vitia superet, adjuvetur, recte pieque vivi non potest a mortalibus.*[23]

67

Yet on the other hand, he was induced to defend the freedom of the will for the following three reasons:

(1) His opposition to the *Manichaeans*,[24] against whom the books *De libero arbitrio* are expressly directed, because they denied free will and assumed a different original source both of evil and bad. He already alludes to them in the last chapter of the book *De quanitate animae*:[25] *Datum est animae liberum arbitrium, quod qui nugatoriis ratiocinationibus labefactare conantur, usque adeo coeci sunt, ut . . .* [26]

(2) The natural delusion, uncovered by me, by virtue of which the "I can do what I will" is regarded as evidence of the freedom of the will, and "*voluntary*" is at once taken to be identical with "*free*." *De*

---

[19] *Revisions.*   [20] *On Nature and Grace.*

[21] "But now the fact is that man is not good and does not have it in his power to be good; either he may not see how he should be, or he does and may not wish to be so."

[22] "Now it may be that from ignorance he does not possess the free decision of the will to choose what he properly should do; or it may be that, by reason of carnal custom, which has been to a certain extent naturally aggravated by mortal sin, he does see how he should act correctly and wishes to do so, but is unable to carry it out."

[23] "Therefore, unless the will itself is freed by divine grace from the bondage by which it has become the servant of sin, and is assisted in overcoming the vices, mortals cannot live righteous and devout lives."

[24] A religious movement named after its founder, the Persian Mani (216–77), who taught a radical dualism of good and evil.

[25] *On the Grandeur of the Soul.*

[26] "The soul is given free decision of choice, and whoever tries to upset this by droll sophistry is so blind that he . . . and so on."

libero arbitrio, I, 12: *Quid enim tam in voluntate, quam ipsa voluntas, situm est?*[27]

(3) The necessity to reconcile the moral responsibility of the human being with the justice of God. For Augustine's keen mind did not overlook an extremely serious difficulty. Its removal is so hard that, as far as I know, all the later philosophers, with the exception of three, whom we shall therefore consider in a moment in more detail, have preferred quietly to creep around it, as if it were nonexistent. Augustine, on the contrary, expresses it quite frankly with noble candor at the very beginning of his books *De libero arbitrio*: *Dic mihi, quaeso, utrum Deus non sit auctor mali?*[28] – And then at greater length immediately in the second chapter: *Movet autem animum, si peccata ex his animabus sunt, quas Deus creavit, illae autem animae ex Deo; quomodo non, parvo intervallo, peccata referantur in Deum.*[29] Whereupon the interlocutor adds: *Id nunc plane abs te dictum est, quod me cogitantem satis excruciat.*[30] – This extremely serious consideration was again taken up by *Luther* and brought into relief with all the vehemence of his eloquence, *De servo arbitrio*, p. 144. *At talem oportere esse Deum, qui LIBERTATE sua NECESSITATEM imponat nobis, ipsa ratio naturalis cogitur confiteri. – Concessa praescientia et omnipotentia, sequitur naturaliter, irrefragabili consequentia, nos per nos ipsos non esse factos, nec vivere, nec agere quidquam, sed per illius omnipotentiam. – Pugnat ex diametro praescientia et omnipotentia Dei cum nostro libero arbitrio. – Omnes homines coguntur inevitabili consequentia admittere, nos non fieri nostra voluntate, sed necessitate; ita nos non facere quod libet, pro jure liberi arbitrii, sed prout Deus praescivit et agit consilio et virtute infallibili et immutabili*, and so on.[31]

---

[27] "For what lies so much in the power of the will as the will itself?"

[28] "Tell me, I pray, whether God is not the author of evil."

[29] "My mind is disturbed by the following question: If sins spring from those souls that God has created, but those souls come from God, how is it possible except for sins to indirectly redound on God?"

[30] "You have now said the very thing that has tormented me not a little in my thoughts."

[31] "Natural reason must already concede that God is bound to be such as to subject us to *necessity* in virtue of his *freedom*. – If we admit omniscience and omnipotence, it naturally follows without question that we are not made, nor do we live and do anything through ourselves, but only through his omnipotence. – God's omniscience and omnipotence flatly contradict the freedom of our will. – All human beings are forced with inevitable consistency to recognize that we become what we are not by our will, but by necessity; that therefore we cannot do what we like by virtue of a freedom of the will, but rather according as God has foreseen it and enacts it by infallible and immutable resolution and will."

At the beginning of the seventeenth century we find *Vanini*[32] entirely imbued with this knowledge. It is the core and soul of his persistent revolt against theism, which had to be concealed as cunningly as possible owing to the pressure of the times. He comes back to it at every opportunity and never wearies of presenting it from the most different points of view. E.g., in his *Amphitheatrum aeternae providentiae, exercitatio* 16, he says: *Si Deus vult peccata, igitur facit: scriptum est enim "omnia quaecunque voluit fecit." Si non vult, tamen committuntur: erit ergo dicendus improvidus, vel impotens, vel crudelis; cum voti sui compos fieri aut nesciat, aut nequeat, aut negligat. – Philosophi inquiunt: si nollet Deus pessimas ac nefarias in orbe vigere actiones, procul dubio uno nutu extra mundi limites omnia flagitia exterminaret, profligaretque: quis enim nostrum divinae potest resistere voluntati? Quomodo invito Deo patrantur scelera, si in actu quoque peccandi scelestis vires subministrat? Ad haec, si contra Dei voluntatem homo labitur, Deus erit inferior homine, qui ei adversatur, et praevalet. Hinc deducunt: Deus ita desiderat hunc mundum, qualis est: si meliorem vellet, meliorem haberet. –* And *exercitatio* 44: *Instrumentum movetur prout a suo principali dirigitur: sed nostra voluntas in suis operationibus se habet tanquam instrumentum, Deus vero ut agens principale: ergo si haec male operatur, Deo imputadum est. – Voluntas nostra non solum quoad motum, sed quoad substantiam quoque tota a Deo dependet: quare nihil est, quod eidem imputari vere possit, neque ex parte substantiae, neque operationis, sed totum Deo, qui voluntatem sic formavit, et ita movet. – Cum essentia et motus voluntatis sit a Deo, adscribi eidem debent vel bonae, vel malae voluntatis operationes, si haec ad illum se habet velut instrumentum.*[33] When reading Vanini, however, we must bear in

69

---

[32] Lucilio Vanini (1584–1619): Italian philosopher. His *Amphitheatrum aeternae providentiae* (*Amphitheater of Divine Providence*) was published in 1615.

[33] Exercise 16: "If God wills sins, he will therefore produce them, for it is written that 'he brings about all that he wills.' If he does not will them and yet they are committed, then we must declare him to be either improvident or not omnipotent or cruel, for then he does not carry out his decree either because he is ignorant or powerless or indolent. – Philosophers say that, if God did not want mean and infamous actions to occur in the world, he would, no doubt, with a nod banish and abolish from the world all scandalous deeds. For who of us could resist the divine will? How could crimes be committed against the will of God, if with every sinful action he endows the criminal with the strength to commit it? Moreover, if a human being sins against the will of God, then God is weaker than the human being, and the human being opposes him and triumphs. The result of all this is that God desires to have the world as it is, and that, if he wanted to have a better world, he would have a better one." Exercise 44: "The instrument is moved just as it is directed by its owner. In its actions, however, our will behaves like an instrument, whereas God behaves like the agent proper. Consequently, if the will acts badly, the fault must be imputed to God. – Our will depends entirely on God not only in respect of its

mind that he generally adopts the artifice of advancing in the person of an opponent his real opinion, which he professes to refute and reject with horror, and of making this opponent substantiate it in a thorough and convincing manner. In his own person he then opposes this opinion with shallow reasons and lame arguments, and then, *tanquam re bene gesta*,[34] goes off in triumph – relying on the malignity of his reader. By this cunning move he deceived even the highly learned Sorbonne, which, taking all this for genuine coin, naively allowed his most godless writings to be published. Its joy was therefore the greater when, three years later, it saw him burnt alive after his blasphemous tongue had been previously cut out. For this after all is the really powerful argument of the theologians, and since it has been taken from them, things have gone seriously wrong for them.

Of philosophers in the stricter sense, *Hume*[35] is, if I am not mistaken, the first who, instead of evading the serious difficulty first raised by Augustine, candidly states it in his essay on *Liberty and Necessity*, without, however, alluding to Augustine or Luther, not to mention Vanini. Toward the end of the essay he says: "The ultimate author of all our volitions is the creator of the world, who first bestowed motion on this immense machine, and placed all beings in that particular position, whence every subsequent event, by an inevitable necessity, must result. Human actions therefore either can have no turpitude at all, as proceeding from so good a cause, or, if they have any turpitude, they must involve *our creator* in the same guilt, while he is acknowledged to be their ultimate cause and author. For as a man, who fired a mine, is answerable for all the consequences whether the train employed be long or short; so wherever a continued chain of necessary causes is fixed, that Being, either finite or infinite, who produces the first, is likewise the author of all the rest." Hume makes an attempt to resolve this difficulty, but in the end admits that he considers it to be insoluble.

70

operation, but also of its substance. Hence there is nothing that could be truly imputed to the will either in respect of its substance or of its operation, but all must be imputed only to God who has thus created the will and sets it in operation. – As the essence and operation of the will emanate from God, the good as well as the bad effects of the will must be attributed to him, if the will is related to him as an instrument."

[34] "As though he had made out a very good case."

[35] David Hume (1711–76): Scottish philosopher, historian, and essayist. His essay "On Liberty and Necessity" is part of *An Enquiry Concerning Human Understanding*, first published in 1748 under the title *Philosophical Essays Concerning the Human Understanding*.

Even *Kant*, independently of his predecessors, runs up against the same stumbling block in the *Critique of Practical Reason*, pp. 180ff. of the fourth edition: "It seems, however, that, as soon as we assume God, as the universal primordial being, to be also the *cause of the existence of substance*, we must admit a human being's actions to have their determining ground in that which is entirely outside his power, namely in the causality of a supreme being that is distinct from his, and on which his existence and the whole determination of his causality entirely depend. – The human being would be a mere Vaucanson's automaton[36] constructed and wound up by the supreme master of all the works of art. Self-consciousness would indeed make it into a

71 thinking automaton, but the consciousness of its spontaneity would be a mere delusion, if such spontaneity were taken to be freedom. For only comparatively does this spontaneity merit being called free, because the nearest determining causes of his movement, and a long series of them leading up to their determining causes, are of course within him, but yet the ultimate and supreme cause lies entirely in the hand of someone else."[37] – Kant attempts to clear up this great difficulty by means of the distinction between thing in itself and appearance; but it is so obvious that this does not alter the essence of the matter in any way that I am convinced he was not in earnest at all. He himself also admits on page 184 the inadequacy of his solution, for he adds: "But is any other solution that has been or may be attempted easier and more comprehensible? On the contrary, it might be said that the dogmatic teachers of metaphysics had shown more *cunning* than candor, for as far as possible they put this difficult point out of sight in the hope that, if nothing at all were said about it, perhaps no one would readily think of it."[38]

After this very remarkable assortment of the most heterogeneous voices, all saying the same thing, I return to our Church Father. The arguments with which he hopes to set aside the difficulty that was already felt by him in all its gravity are theological, not philosophical, and so are not of unconditional validity. As I have said, supporting those arguments is the third of the above-mentioned reasons for his attempting to defend a *liberum arbitrium* with which God has endowed the human being. Such a *liberum arbitrium*, interposing itself between

---

[36] An automated machine named after the French inventor Jacques Vaucanson (1709–82).
[37] Academy edition, v, 100.   [38] Ibid., 103.

72 the Creator and the sins of his creature, would really suffice to remove the whole difficulty, since it is easily said in words and may be enough perhaps for thought that does not go much beyond these, if only it might also remain at least *conceivable* on serious and deeper reflection. But how are we to picture to ourselves a being which, in respect of its whole *existentia* and *essentia*, is the work of another, and is yet able to determine itself primarily, originally, and fundamentally, and accordingly be responsible for its actions? The proposition *operari sequitur esse*, i.e., that the effects of every being follow from its constitution, upsets that assumption, but is itself irrefutable. If a human being's conduct is bad, then this is so because he is bad. But to that proposition is attached its corollary: *ergo unde esse, inde operari.*[39] What should we say of the watchmaker who was angry with his watch because it was off? However much we may like to make a *tabula rasa* of the will, we cannot help admitting that, if, e.g., one of two human beings follows a course of action the very opposite to that of the other in a moral respect, this difference, which must nevertheless spring from somewhere, has its ground either in the external circumstances, in which case guilt obviously does not attach to human beings, or in an original difference of their will itself, in which case again guilt and merit do not attach to them if their whole being and essence are the work of another. After the above-mentioned great men tried in vain to find a way out of this labyrinth, I readily confess that to think of moral responsibility of the human will without the latter's aseity[40] is also beyond my power of comprehension. It was undoubtedly the same inability that dictated the seventh of the eight definitions with which *Spinoza*[41] opens his *Ethica*: *Ea res libera dicetur, quae ex sola naturae suae necessitate existit, et a se sola ad agendum determinatur; necessaria autem, vel potius coacta, quae ab alio determinatur ad existendum et operandum.*[42]

Thus if a bad action springs from the nature, i.e., from the inborn constitution of a human being, then the guilt obviously lies on the author and creator of that nature. Therefore free will was invented. But

---

[39] "Consequently, where the being is from, there also comes the doing."

[40] German *Aseität*, from Latin *aseitas*: being self-originated and hence absolutely independent of anything.

[41] Baruch Spinoza (1632–77): Dutch philosopher of Portuguese Jewish descent. His *Ethica* (*Ethics*) was published posthumously in 1677.

[42] "That thing must be called free which exists only from the necessity of its own nature and is determined by itself alone to act. But that thing is called necessary, or rather constrained, which is determined by another to exist and act."

on its assumption, it is absolutely impossible to see from what that bad action is supposed to spring, since free will is at bottom a merely *negative* quality and simply states that nothing compels the human being to act in such-and-such a way or prevents him from so acting. But in this way, it never becomes clear *from where* the action ultimately springs, for it is not supposed to proceed from the inborn or implanted disposition of the human being, since the guilt would then fall upon his Creator. Nor is the guilt to proceed from the external circumstances alone, since it would then be attributable to chance, and so the human being would in any case remain innocent – though he is nevertheless made responsible for it. The natural image of a free will is an empty set of scales. It hangs there at rest and will never lose its equilibrium unless something is laid on one of the pans. Free will can no more produce an action out of itself than the scale can produce a movement of itself, since nothing comes from nothing. If the set of scales is to go down to one side, a foreign body must be laid on it, and this is then the source of the movement. In the same way, human action must be brought forth by something that operates *positively* and is more than a mere *negative* freedom. But this can happen in only two ways: either it is done by the motives in and by themselves, i.e., by the external circumstances; the human being is then obviously not responsible for the action, and moreover all human beings in the same circumstances would then inevitably act in precisely the same way; or it springs from his susceptibility to such motives and thus from the inborn character, i.e., from the inclinations originally inherent in the human being. These inclinations may be different in individuals, and by virtue of them the motives operate. But then the will is no longer free, for those inclinations are the weight laid on the pan. The responsibility falls on him who laid them there, i.e., on him whose work is the human being with such inclinations. And so the human being is responsible for his doing only in the case where he himself is his own work, i.e., where he has aseity.

The whole point of view on the matter expounded here enables us to see how much depends on the freedom of the will, which forms an unremovable gulf between the Creator and the sins of his creature. From this it is easy to understand why the theologians stick to it so persistently, and why their shield-bearers, the professors of philosophy, support them, as in duty bound, with such zeal that, deaf and blind to

73

the most conclusive proofs to the contrary of great thinkers, they cling to free will and fight for it as *pro ara et focis*.[43]

74   But finally, to conclude my account of *Augustine*, which was previously interrupted; his opinion on the whole amounts to this, that only before the Fall did the human being really have an absolutely free will, but that thereafter he became tainted with original sin, and must hope for his salvation through predestination and redemption – an utterance sounding like that of a Church Father.

Meanwhile, it is through *Augustine* and his dispute with the Manichaeans and Pelagians that philosophy awoke to an awareness of our problem. Thereafter, through the scholastic philosophers, it gradually became clearer to philosophy, and *Buridan's* sophism and the above-mentioned passage from *Dante* are evidence of this. – But the first to go thoroughly into the matter was apparently *Thomas Hobbes*. His work, *Quaestiones de libertate et necessitate, contra Doctorem Branhallum*, published in 1656 was specially devoted to this subject.[44] It is now scarce and is found in English in a folio volume entitled *Th. Hobbes: Moral and Political Works*, London, 1750, pp. 469ff. I quote the following main passage from this. P. 483:

"(6) Nothing takes a beginning from itself; but from the action of some other immediate agent, without itself. Therefore, when first a man has an appetite or will to something, to which immediately before he had no appetite nor will; the cause of his will is not the will itself, but something else not in his own disposing. So that, whereas it is out of controversy, that of voluntary actions the will is the necessary cause, and by this which is said, the will is also necessarily *caused* by other things, whereof it disposes not, it follows that voluntary actions have all of them necessary causes, and therefore are *necessitated*.

"(7) I hold *that* to be a *sufficient* cause, to which nothing is wanting that is needful to the producing of the *effect*. The same is also a *necessary* cause: for, if it be possible that a *sufficient* cause shall not bring forth the *effect*, then there wanteth something, which was needful to the producing of it; and so the cause was not *sufficient*. But if it be impossible that a *sufficient* cause should not produce the effect; then is a

---

[43] "For hearth and home."

[44] An English version of Hobbes's *Quaestiones de libertate et necessitate, contra Doctorem Branhallum* (*Questions on Liberty and Necessity, Against Dr. Bramhall*) was published in 1656 under the title *The Questions Concerning Liberty, Necessity, and Chance. Clearly Stated and Debated Between Dr. Bramhall Bishop of Derry and Thomas Hobbes of Malmesbury.*

sufficient cause a *necessary* cause. Hence it is manifest, that whatever is produced, is produced *necessarily*. For whatsoever is produced has had a *sufficient* cause to produce it, or else it had not been: and therefore also *voluntary* actions are *necessitated*.

"(8) That ordinary definition of a free agent (namely that a free agent is that, which, when all things are present, which are needful to produce the effect, can nevertheless not produce it) implies a contradiction and is Nonsense; being as much as to say, the cause may be *sufficient*, that is to say *necessary*, and yet the effect shall not follow." –

P. 485: "Every accident, how contingent soever it seem, or how *voluntary* soever it be, is produced *necessarily*."

In his famous book *De cive*,[45] c. 1, § 7, he says: *Fertur unusquisque ad appetitionem ejus, quod sibi bonum, et ad fugam ejus, quod sibi malum est, maxime autem maximi malorum naturalium, quae est mors; idque necessitate quadam naturae non minore, quam qua fertur lapis deorsum.*[46]

Immediately after *Hobbes* we see *Spinoza* imbued with the same conviction. A few passages will suffice to characterize his teaching on this point:

Ethica, pt. I, prop. 32: *Voluntas non potest vocari causa libera, sed tantum necessaria.*[47] – Coroll. 2: *Nam voluntas, ut reliqua omnia, causa indiget, a qua ad operandum certo modo determinatur.*[48]

Ibid., pt. II, prop. 49. Schol.: *Quod denique ad quartam objectionem (de Buridani asina) attinet, dico, me omnino concedere, quod homo in tali aequilibrio positus (nempe qui nihil aliud percipit quam sitim et famem, talem cibum et talem potum, qui aeque ab eo distant) fame et siti peribit.*[49]

Ibid., pt. III, prop. 2. Schol.: *Mentis decreta eadem necessitate in mente oriuntur, ac ideae rerum actu existentium. Qui igitur credunt, se ex libero mentis decreto loqui vel tacere, vel quidquam agere, oculis apertis som-*

---

[45] Literally, *The Citizen*. The Latin version was published in 1642, the English version in 1651 under the title *Philosophical Rudiments Concerning Government and Society*.

[46] "Everyone is urged to desire what is good for him, and to flee from what is bad for him, but most of all from that which is the greatest of all natural evils, namely death. And this happens by virtue of a natural necessity as great as that by virtue of which a stone falls to the ground."

[47] "The will cannot be called a free but only a necessary cause."

[48] "For, just like everything else, the will needs a cause whereby it is determined to exist and act in a definite way."

[49] "Finally, as regards the fourth objection (of Buridan's ass). I am quite ready to admit that, if a human being found himself in such a position of equilibrium (namely where he perceived nothing but hunger and thirst, and a certain food and a certain drink were each equidistant from him) he would inevitably die of hunger and thirst."

niant.[50] – Letter LVIII to Schuller: *Unaquaeque res necessario a causa externa aliqua determinatur ad existendum et operandum certa ac determinata ratione. Ex. gr. lapis a causa externa, ipsum impellente, certam motus quantitatem accipit, qua postea moveri necessario perget. Concipe jam lapidem, dum moveri pergit, cogitare et scire, se, quantum potest, conari, ut moveri pergat. Hic sane lapis, quandoquidem sui tantummodo conatus est conscius et minime indifferens, se liberrimum esse et nulla alia de causa in motu perseverare credet, quam quia vult. Atque haec humana illa libertas est, quam omnes habere jactant, et quae in hoc solo consistit, quod homines sui appetitus sint conscii, et causarum, a quibus determinantur, ignari. – His, quaenam mea de libera et coacta necessitate, deque ficta humana libertate sit sententia, satis explicui.*[51]

77   But it is a remarkable circumstance that *Spinoza* reached this insight only in the last years of his life (in his forties). For previously, in 1665, when he was still a Cartesian, he had resolutely and vigorously defended the opposite opinion in his *Cogitata metaphysica*,[52] II, c. 12, and even, in flat contradiction to the *scholium* of *Ethica*, pt. II, prop. 49 just mentioned, had said with regard to Buridan's sophism: *Si enim hominem loco asinae ponamus in tali aequilibrio positum, homo, non pro re cogitante, sed pro turpissimo asino erit habendus, si fame et siti pereat.*[53]

Later on I shall have to report the same change of opinion and conversion in the case of two other great men. This indicates how difficult and deeply hidden the correct insight into our problem is.

In his essay on *Liberty and Necessity*, from which I had to quote a passage previously, *Hume* writes with the clearest conviction about the

---

[50] "The decisions of the mind arise in the mind with the same necessity as do the ideas of the things that exist in reality. Therefore whoever believes that he speaks, or keeps silent, or does anything else from the free decision of his mind dreams with his eyes open."

[51] "Each thing is necessarily determined by some external cause to exist and operate in a certain and determined way. For example, the stone receives a definite quantum of motion from an external cause that pushes it, by virtue of which it must necessarily continue to move. Now assume that the stone, while continuing to move, thinks and is conscious of striving with all its force to continue in motion. Then, as this stone is conscious only of its striving and is by no means indifferent to it, it will believe itself to be entirely free and to continue moving from no other cause than that it wills to move. And so it is with that human freedom which all boast of having, and which consists only in the fact that human beings are conscious only of their willing, and ignore the causes by which they are determined. – Thus I have sufficiently explained what I think of free and forced necessity and of the imaginary freedom of the human being."

[52] *Thoughts on Metaphysics*; forms the appendix to Spinoza's *Renati des Cartes principiorum philosophiae* (*The Principles of Descartes' Philosophy*) published in 1665.

[53] "For if we assume that a human being instead of an ass were in such a position of equilibrium, the human being would be regarded as a thoroughly stupid ass, and not as a thinking human being, if he were to die of hunger and thirst."

necessity of individual acts of will when the motives are given, and states this most distinctly in his thoroughly intelligible manner. He says: "Thus it appears that the conjunction between motives and voluntary actions is as regular and uniform as that between the cause and effect in any part of nature." And further he says: "It seems almost impossible, therefore, to engage either in science or action of any kind, without acknowledging the doctrine of necessity and this inference from motives to voluntary actions, from character to conduct."

78 But no author has demonstrated the necessity of acts of will so extensively and convincingly as *Priestley* has in his work, *The Doctrine of Philosophical Necessity*,[54] which is exclusively devoted to this subject. Whoever is not convinced by this exceedingly clear and comprehensible book must have an understanding that is really paralyzed by prejudices. To characterize his results, I quote a few passages from the second edition, Birmingham 1782:

Preface, p. xx: "There is no absurdity more glaring to my understanding, than the notion of philosophical liberty." – P. 26: "Without a miracle, or the intervention of some foreign cause, no volition or action of any man could have been otherwise, than it has been." – P. 37: "Though an inclination or affection of mind be not gravity, it influences me and acts upon me as certainly and necessarily, as this power does upon a stone." – P. 43: "Saying that the will is *self-determined*, gives no idea at all, or rather implies an absurdity, namely that a *determination*, which is an *effect*, takes place, without any cause at all. For exclusive of every thing that comes under the denomination of *motive*, there is really nothing at all left, to produce the determination. Let a man use what *words* he pleases, he can have no more a *conception* of how we can sometimes be determined by motives, and sometimes without any motive, than he can have of a scale being sometimes weighed down by weights, and sometimes by a kind of substance that has no weight at all, which, whatever it be in itself, must, with respect to the scale be *nothing*." – P. 66: "In proper philosophical language, the motive ought to be call'd the *proper cause* of the action. It is as much so as any thing in nature is the cause of any thing else." – P. 84: "It will never be in our power to choose two things, when all the previous circumstances are the very same." – P. 90: "A man indeed, when he reproaches himself

---

[54] Priestley's *The Doctrine of Philosophical Necessity Illustrated* is the appendix to his *Disquisitions Relating to Matter and Spirit* published in 1777.

for any particular action in his past conduct, may fancy that, if he was in the same situation again, he would have acted differently. But this is a mere *deception*; and if he examines himself strictly, and takes in all circumstances, he may be satisfied that, with the same inward disposition of mind, and with precisely the same view of things, that he had then, and exclusive of all others, that he has acquired by reflection *since*, he could not have acted otherwise than he did." – P. 287: "In short, there is no choice in the case, but the doctrine of necessity or absolute nonsense."

Now it is to be noted that it was precisely the same with *Priestley* as with *Spinoza* and with yet another very great man who is to be mentioned in a moment. For in the preface to the first edition, p. xxvii, *Priestley* says: "I was not however a ready convert to the doctrine of necessity. Like Dr. Hartley[55] himself, I gave up my liberty with great reluctance, and in a long correspondence which I once had on the subject, I maintained very strenuously the doctrine of liberty, and did not at all yield to the arguments then proposed to me."

The third great man to have found himself in the same situation is *Voltaire*,[56] and he tells us about his conversion in his own characteristically frank and friendly manner. Thus in his *Traité de métaphysique*,[57] chap. 7, he had thoroughly and vigorously defended the so-called freedom of the will. But in his book, *Le philosophe ignorant*,[58] written more than forty years later, he teaches the strict necessitation of acts of will in chapter 13, which he ends with the following words: *Archimède est également nécessité à rester dans sa chambre, quand on l'y enferme, et quand il est si fortement occupé d'un problème, qu'il ne reçoit pas l'idée de sortir:*

Ducunt volentem fata, nolentem trahunt.

L'IGNORANT QUI PENSE AINSI N'A PAS TOUJOURS PENSÉ DE MÊME, mais il est enfin contraint de se rendre.[59] In the next

79

80

---

55 David Hartley (1705–57): English philosopher and physician.
56 Voltaire, pen name of François-Marie Arouet (1694–1778): French man of letters and philosopher.
57 *Treatise in Metaphysics*, published in 1734.
58 *The Philosopher Without Knowledge*, published in 1766.
59 "Archimedes is compelled with equal necessity to remain in his room when he is locked in, as when he is so deeply engrossed in a problem that he does not think of going out:
The willing is led, the unwilling dragged by fate. [Seneca, *Epist.*, 107, 11]
The fool who thinks thus has not always thought the same; but in the end he was compelled to surrender."

book, *Le principe d'action*,[60] he says in chapter 13: *Une boule, qui en pousse une autre, un chien de chasse, qui court nécessairement et volontairement après un cerf, ce cerf, qui franchit un fossé immense avec non moins de nécessité et de volonté: tout cela n'est pas plus invinciblement déterminé que nous le sommes à tout ce que nous fesons.*[61]

This equal conversion to our insight by three such eminent minds must certainly perplex anyone who undertakes to dispute well-established truths with the wholly irrelevant "I can do what I will" of his simple self-consciousness.

81   After these immediate predecessors of *Kant*, we must not be surprised that he regarded as a foregone conclusion with others as well as himself the necessity with which the empirical character is determined through motives to actions, and that he did not stop to demonstrate it afresh. His *Idea for a Universal History* begins: "Whatever one's conception in a metaphysical regard of *the freedom of the will*, the *appearances* of it, human actions, are just as much determined by universal laws of nature as is every other natural event."[62] – In the *Critique of Pure Reason* (p. 548 of the first edition or p. 577 of the fifth)[63] he says: "Since this empirical character itself must be drawn from the appearance as effect, and from the rule of it provided by experience, all actions of a human being in the appearance are determined in accordance with the order of nature from his empirical character and the cooperating other causes. If we could thoroughly examine all appearances of his power of choice, there would not be a single human action which we could not predict with certainty, and know as necessary from its antecedent conditions. Therefore as regards this empirical character, there is no freedom, and yet it is solely with respect to the empirical character that we can regard the human being, if we only *observe* and wish to investigate physiologically from his

---

[60] The complete title is *Il faut prendre un parti ou Le principe d'action* (*One Has to Choose Sides, or The Principle of Action*), published in 1772.

[61] "A ball that strikes another; a hunting dog that necessarily and voluntarily chases a stag; this stag which jumps just as necessarily and voluntarily a wide ditch – all this is just as irresistibly determined as are we in all that we do."

[62] The complete title of Kant's essay is *Idea for a Universal History with a Cosmopolitan Purpose* (*Idee zu einer allgemeinen Geschichte in weltbürgerlicher Absicht*), published in 1784. Schopenhauer is quoting the first sentence of the work.

[63] The paginations of the first and fifth editions of the *Critique of Pure Resson* which Schopenhauer provides here and in subsequent citations of the *Critique* coincide with the A and B pagination, respectively, indicated in the modern English translations of the work.

actions the causes that prompt them, as is done in anthropology." – Again on p. 798 of the first edition or p. 826 of the fifth, he says: "The will indeed may be free, but this can concern only the intelligible cause of our willing. For as regards the phenomena of its manifestations, i.e., the actions, we must always explain them as we do all the other phenomena of nature, namely in accordance with unchangeable laws. An inviolable fundamental maxim without which we cannot make any empirical use of our faculty of reason obliges us to do this." Again in the *Critique of Practical Reason*, p. 177 of the fourth edition: "We can therefore concede that, if it were possible for us to have so deep an insight into a human being's way of thinking, as revealed by inner as well as outer actions, that every spring of action, even the smallest, were known to us, likewise all the external occasions influencing it, we could calculate his future conduct with the same certainty as we can an eclipse of the moon or sun."[64]

But associated with this is Kant's doctrine of the coexistence of freedom with necessity by virtue of the distinction between the intelligible and the empirical characters. As I entirely subscribe to this view, I shall later return to it. *Kant* has twice expounded it, in the *Critique of Pure Reason*, pp. 532–54 of the first edition or pp. 560–82 of the fifth, but even more clearly in the *Critique of Practical Reason*, pp. 169–79 of the fourth edition or pp. 224–31 of Rosenkranz's.[65] These exceedingly profound passages must be read by everyone who wishes to attain a thorough knowledge of the compatibility of human freedom with necessity. –

Thus far the present treatment of the subject differs from the achievements of all these noble and venerable predecessors in two main points. In the first place, as directed by the prize question, I have clearly separated the inner perception of the will in self-consciousness from the outer, and have considered each by itself; in this way, it has first become possible to discover the source of that deception which has so irresistible an effect on most people. Secondly, I have taken into consideration the will in connection with all the rest of nature, which no one before me has done, and thus it was first possible to treat the subject with the thoroughness, methodical insight, and completeness of which it is susceptible.

82

---

[64] Academy edition, v, 99.   [65] See ibid., 94–100.

Now we still have a few words to say about some authors who wrote after *Kant*; but I do not regard them as my predecessors.

In his *Philosophische Untersuchungen über das Wesen der menschlichen Freiheit*, pp. 465–71,[66] *Schelling* furnished an explanatory paraphrase of *Kant's* highly important doctrine regarding the intelligible and empirical characters, a doctrine that I have just commended. By the vividness of its color, this paraphrase may make the matter clearer to many than Kant's thorough but dry exposition. But I cannot mention it without reproving *Schelling* out of respect for truth and Kant. For he states one of the most important, most admirable, and, in my opinion, most profound of all the Kantian doctrines, but he does not say clearly and expressly that what he is expounding belongs in terms of its content to *Kant*. On the contrary, he so expresses himself that most readers, not intimately acquainted with the content of the great man's detailed and difficult works, are bound to think that here they are reading *Schelling's* own thoughts. Here I will only show by *one* of many instances how the result served his purpose. Even at the present time, Herr Erdmann,[67] a young professor of philosophy in Halle, says in his book, *Leib und Seele*, 1837, p. 101: "Although Leibniz, like Schelling in his treatise on freedom, represents the soul as determining itself prior to all time," and so on. Thus *Schelling* here stands to *Kant* in the fortunate relation of *Amerigo* to *Columbus*; another man's discovery is labeled with his name. For this, however, he is indebted not to chance, but to his own shrewdness. For he begins on p. 465: "Indeed it is only *idealism* that has raised the doctrine of freedom to that plane,"[68] etc., and then follow immediately the Kantian thoughts. Thus instead of honestly saying here *Kant*, he cleverly says *idealism*. But by this ambiguous expression everyone will here understand *Fichte's*[69] philosophy and *Schelling's* first, i.e., Fichtean, philosophy, not *Kant's* teaching. For the latter had protested against the naming of his philosophy as *idealism* (e.g., *Prolegomena*, p. 51),[70] and had even inserted a "refutation of idealism" in his second edition of the *Critique of Pure*

---

[66] See F. W. J. Schelling, *Philosophical Inquiries into the Nature of Human Freedom*, trans. James Gutmann (La Salle, IL: Open Court, 1989), 61–66.

[67] Johann Eduard Erdmann (1805–92): German philosopher and historian of philosophy. *Body and Soul* was published in 1837.

[68] See *Philosophical Inquiries*, 61.

[69] Johann Gottlieb Fichte (1762–1814): German philosopher. Follower of Kant. Schopenhauer attended his lectures in Berlin in 1812–13.

[70] See Academy edition, IV, 293.

Reason, p. 274. On the following page *Schelling* very cleverly mentions in an incidental phrase the "Kantian concept" in order to appease those who already know that it is the Kantian riches that he is here so pompously displaying as his own merchandise. But then on p. 472,[71] in defiance of all truth and justice, it is said that *Kant* had *not* risen to that view in his theory, etc.; whereas from the two immortal passages of *Kant* previously recommended by me for perusal, everyone can clearly see that precisely this view belongs originally to him alone, and without him thousands of minds like those of Messrs. *Fichte and Schelling* would never have been capable of grasping it. Since I had to speak here of *Schelling's* treatise, I was not permitted to keep silent on this point, but have fulfilled only my duty to that great teacher of humankind who alone along with *Goethe* is the just pride of the German nation by returning to him what incontestably belongs to him alone – and this especially in an age to which *Goethe's* words, "The boys are masters of the course,"[72] are peculiarly applicable. – Moreover, in the same treatise *Schelling* was just as ready to appropriate the thoughts, and even the very words, of *Jacob Böhme*[73] without disclosing their source.

Except for this paraphrase of Kant's thoughts, those "inquiries concerning freedom"[74] contain nothing that could help furnish us with fresh or thorough information on the topic. This is also indicated at the very beginning from the definition of freedom as "a faculty of good and evil." Such a definition may be suitable for the catechism, but in philosophy it means nothing and consequently nothing can be done with it. For good and evil are far from being simple concepts (*notiones simplices*) that would be clear in themselves and need no explanation, determination, and justification. In general only a small part of that treatise deals with freedom; rather, its principal contents are a detailed account of a God with whom the worthy author betrays an intimate acquaintance, for he even describes to us his coming about. It is only to be regretted that he does not say a word on how he arrived at such an acquaintance. The beginning of the treatise consists of a tissue of sophisms, and anyone will recognize their shallowness who is not to be overawed by the audacity of the tone.

[71] See *Philosophical Inquiries*, 67.
[72] From Goethe's poem *Parabolic*, no. 7, line 8 (*Parabolisch*, no. 7, line 8).
[73] Jakob Böhme (1575–1624): German Lutheran mystic, cobbler, and merchant.
[74] Schelling's previously cited and quoted work.

85 Since that piece and in consequence of it and similar productions, the place of clear concepts and honest inquiry in German philosophy has been taken by "intellectual intuition" and "absolute thinking"; posturing, puzzling, mystifying, throwing dust in the reader's eyes by all manner of tricks have become the method, and self-seeking instead of truth-seeking[75] governs what is said by lecturers. Through all this, philosophy, if we can still so call it, was bound to sink lower and lower until it ultimately reached the lowest depth of degradation in that ministerial creature, *Hegel*.[76] To stifle once more the freedom of thought gained by *Kant*, *Hegel* turned philosophy, the daughter of reason and future mother of truth, into a tool for the purposes of the state and for obscurantism and protestant Jesuitism. To disguise the scandal and at the same time bring about the greatest possible stultification of people's minds, he threw over it a cloak of the hollowest display of words and of the most senseless gibberish that has ever been heard, outside a lunatic asylum at any rate.

In England and France philosophy stands on the whole almost exactly where *Locke* and *Condillac*[77] left it. *Maine de Biran*,[78] called by his editor, M. *Cousin*, *le premier métaphysicien français de mon tems*,[79] is a fanatical exponent of the *liberum arbitrium indifferentiae* in his *Nouvelles considérations du physique et moral*,[80] 1834, and takes it to be something that is absolutely self-evident. The same thing is done by many modern philosophical scribblers in Germany, for whom the *liberum arbitrium indifferentiae* appears under the name of "moral freedom" as a settled thing, just as if all the above-mentioned great men had never existed. They declare the freedom of the will to be given immediately in self-consciousness and thus so firmly established that all arguments against it could be nothing but sophisms. This sublime assurance springs merely from the fact that these good people do not in the least know what freedom of the will is and signifies, but in their innocence understand by it nothing but the sovereign control of the will over the members of the body, which we analyzed in the second section of this

---

[75] The German terms are *Absicht* and *Einsicht*, respectively.
[76] Friedrich Georg Wilhelm Hegel (1770–1831): German philosopher. The dominant philosopher during the middle years of Schopenhauer's life.
[77] Etienne Bonnot de Condillac (1715–80): French philosopher and Catholic priest.
[78] François Pierre Maine de Biran (1766–1824): French philosopher and politician.
[79] "The leading French metaphysician of my time."
[80] *New Considerations of the Physical and the Mental.*

essay – a control which no reasonable human being has ever doubted, and whose expression is just the "I can do what I will." They quite honestly imagine this to be the freedom of the will, and boast that it is beyond all doubt. It is this very state of innocence into which the Hegelian philosophy, after so many great predecessors, has put back the thinking mind of Germany. Of course to people of this description we could exclaim:

> "Are ye not like women who return
> And yet again return to their first word,
> Though we reason with them for hours?"[81]

However, it may be that many of them are secretly influenced by the theological motives previously mentioned.

And again, see how our present-day writers on medicine, zoology, history, politics, and *belles lettres* are most eager to seize every opportunity for mentioning "human freedom," "moral freedom"! They are somewhat conceited about it. Of course they do not enter into any explanation. But if we could examine them, we should find that they either think of nothing at all with it or think of our old, honorable, well-known *liberum arbitrium indifferentiae*, no matter what fine phrases they might clothe it in. Now this is a concept about whose inadmissibility no one will ever succeed in convincing the masses, yet about which scholars should beware of talking with such innocence. For this reason, there are among them a few with faint hearts who are very amusing, since they no longer venture to talk about the freedom of the *will*, but say instead "freedom of the *spirit*," to make it sound refined, and with this they hope to get by. To the discerning reader who asks me what they mean by this, I am fortunately able to answer: Nothing, absolutely nothing; it is just a vague and really meaningless expression in the good old German fashion, which gives to their vacuity and faintheartedness a welcome hiding place to enable them to make their escape. The word "spirit" is really a figurative expression, and always denotes *intellectual* abilities in contrast to the will. These, however, are certainly not supposed to be free in their action, but are supposed to accommodate themselves and are subject first to the rules of logic and then to the *object* of cognition in each case, so that they apprehend

[81] The verses are by the German dramatist, poet, historian, and philosopher Friedrich Schiller (1759–1805), and come from act II, sc. 3, of *Wallensteins Tod* (*The Death of Wallenstein*), the final part of the dramatic trilogy *Wallenstein*, published in 1800.

purely, i.e., *objectively*, and it is never a case of *stat pro ratione voluntas*.[82] In general this "spirit," which is found everywhere in the German literature of today, is a highly suspicious fellow, and we should therefore ask for his passport whenever we come across him. Its most frequent business is to serve as a mask for the poverty of thoughts associated with faintheartedness. Moreover it is well known that the German word for *spirit* (*Geist*) is cognate with the word gas, which, coming from the Arabic and alchemy, signifies vapor or air, just as do *spiritus*, πνεῦμα, *animus*. *Animus* is cognate with ἄνεμος (wind).

With regard to our theme, such then is the state of affairs in the philosophical world and in the wider scholarly world, after all that the above-mentioned great minds have taught about it. This once more confirms the fact that not only has nature at all times produced extremely few genuine thinkers as rare exceptions, but also that these few have themselves always existed only for the very few. This is the reason why folly and error always assert their reign. –

In the case of a moral subject, the testimony of the great poets is also of importance. They do not speak after a systematic investigation, but human nature lies open to their penetrating insight; and so their utterances directly hit on the truth. – In *Shakespeare's Measure for Measure*, act II, sc. 2, Isabella begs the regent Angelo for mercy on behalf of her brother, who had been condemned to death:

> *Angelo.* I will not do it.
> *Isb.* But can you, if you would?
> *Ang.* Look, what I *will* not, that I *cannot* do.

In *Twelfth Night*, act II, we read:

> Fate, show thy force, ourselves we do not owe,
> What is decree'd must be, and be this so.

88   *Walter Scott*,[83] that great judge and portrayer of the human heart and its most secret emotions, has also brought to light this profound truth in his *Saint Ronan's Well*, vol. III, chap. 6. He is describing a repentant sinner who on her deathbed tries to relieve her troubled conscience by confession, and among other things he makes her say:

"Go, and leave me to my fate; I am the most detestable wretch, that

---

[82] "The wish exempts me from giving reasons" (Juvenal, *Satires*, 6, 223).
[83] Sir Walter Scott (1771–1832): Scottish author of historical novels. *Saint Ronan's Well*, published in 1823, is his only novel set in contemporary society.

ever liv'd – detestable to myself, worst of all; because even in my penitence there is a secret whisper that tells me, that were I as I have been, I would again act over all the wickedness I have done, and much worse. Oh! for Heaven's assistance, to crush the wicked thought!''

A proof of *this* poetic description is furnished by the following parallel fact, which at the same time most emphatically confirms the doctrine regarding the constancy of character. It appeared in *The Times* of 2 July 1845, and came from the French paper *La Presse*. The heading is: Military Execution at Oran. "On 24 March the Spaniard Aguilar, *alias* Gomez, had been condemned to death. On the day before the execution, he said in conversation with his jailer: 'I am not so guilty as I have been represented; I am accused of having committed thirty murders, whereas I have committed only twenty-six. From childhood I thirsted for blood; at the age of seven and a half I stabbed a child. I murdered a pregnant woman, and in later years a Spanish officer. In consequence I was forced to flee from Spain. I fled to France where I committed two crimes before I joined the Foreign Legion. Of all my crimes the one I most regret is the following. In 1841, at the head of my company, I captured a deputy commissary general who was escorted by a sergeant, a corporal, and seven men. I had them all beheaded. The death of these men weighs heavily on me; I see them in my dreams, and tomorrow I shall see them in the soldiers detailed to shoot me. *Nevertheless, if I again obtained my liberty, I would go on murdering people.*' ''

The following passages in *Goethe's Iphigenia* (act IV, sc. 2) also has a bearing on the subject:

> *Arcas.* For you have not heeded sincere advice.
> *Iphigenia.* What I could do, I gladly did.
> *Arcas.* It still is not too late to change your mind.
> *Iphigenia. Never is this within our power.*

A famous passage from Schiller's *Wallenstein*[84] also expresses our fundamental truth:

> "Know that man's deeds and thoughts
> Are not like the blind play of ocean waves.
> The inner world, his microcosm, is
> The deep shaft from which they spring eternally.
>
> [84] *Wallenstein's Death*, act II, sc. 3.

Necessary they are, like the fruit of the tree,
Juggling chance can change them not.
When first I have searched man's heart,
Then do I know his willing and his acts."

V
Conclusion and higher view

It has been a pleasure to recall all those illustrious predecessors, poets as well as philosophers, who have maintained the truth I am advocating. Not authorities, however, but reasons are the philosopher's weapons. I have therefore conducted my case with these alone. Yet I hope to have provided such evidence for it that I am now justified in drawing the conclusion *a non posse ad non esse*.[1] In this way, the negative reply to the question set by the Royal Society, that was established directly and actually, and hence *a posteriori*, above with the investigation of self-consciousness, is now also established indirectly and *a priori*. For that which does not exist at all cannot have in self-consciousness data from which it could be demonstrated.

Now although the truth here advocated may be one of those that might be contrary to the preconceived opinions of the short-sighted masses, and indeed offensive to the feeble and ignorant, this could not stop me from expounding it without equivocation and reserve. For here I am speaking not to the people but to an enlightened academy, which has set its very timely question not for the confirmation of prejudice, but for the honor of truth. – Moreover, so long as it is still a case of establishing and substantiating a truth, the honest seeker of it will always pay attention solely to its reasons and not to its consequences, for there will be time to turn to the latter when the truth itself is established. To test the arguments alone, regardless of the consequences, and not first ask whether or not a recognized truth is in harmony with the system of all our other convictions – this is what

---

[1] "From what cannot be to what is not."

Kant already recommends, and here I cannot refrain from repeating his words: "This confirms the maxim, already acknowledged and commended by others, that in every scientific investigation we should pursue our course undisturbed with all possible precision and openness without worrying whether our investigation might possibly be contrary to anything outside its field; and that, as far as we are able, we should carry it out faithfully and completely for itself alone. Frequent observation has convinced me that, when this business has been carried out to the end, that which in the middle sometimes seemed to me very doubtful in respect of other outside doctrines, finally agreed entirely in an unexpected way with what had been found of itself without the least regard for those doctrines, without partiality and preference for them. This agreement resulted when I ignored those doubts and concentrated on my task till it was complete. Authors would spare themselves many errors and much wasted effort (spent on delusions), if only they could make up their minds to go to work somewhat more frankly and openly" (*Critique of Practical Reason*, p. 190 of the fourth edition).[2]

Our metaphysical cognitions in general are still very far from being so certain that we should reject some solidly grounded truth because its consequences do not tally with the former. On the contrary, every hard-won and established truth is a piece of territory conquered from the domain of the problems of knowledge. It is a fixed point for placing levers that will move other loads; in fact, in favorable instances, we soar all at once from this to a view of the whole that is higher than the one we have had hitherto. For in every sphere of knowledge the concatenation of truths is so great that, whoever has come into the complete possession of a single one, may at all events hope to go on and conquer the whole. In a difficult algebraical problem a single positively given quantity is of inestimable value because it renders possible the solution. In the same way, in the hardest of all human problems, which is metaphysics, the certain knowledge, demonstrated *a priori* and *a posteriori*, of the strict necessity with which actions result from a given character and given motives is such an inestimable datum; starting from it alone, we may arrive at the solution to the whole problem. Therefore all that cannot produce a sound scientific verification must yield when it stands in the way of such a well-established truth; not vice versa. In no

92

---

[2] Academy edition, v, 106.

circumstances should a truth stoop to accommodations and limitations in order to be in harmony with unproved and possibly erroneous assertions.

Here I may be permitted to make yet another general remark. A review of our result leads me to observe that, as regards the two problems already designated in the preceding section as the deepest problems in modern philosophy but of which the ancients were not clearly aware – I mean the problem of the freedom of the will and that of the relation between the ideal and the real – ordinary but untutored common sense is not merely incompetent, but it even has a decided natural tendency to error. To reclaim it from the latter requires a philosophy that is already far advanced. Thus with regard to *knowing*, it is really natural for ordinary common sense to attribute far too much to the *object*; and so it needed *Locke* and *Kant* to show how much of it springs from the *subject*. With regard to *willing*, on the other hand, ordinary common sense has a tendency to attribute far too little to the *object* and far too much to the *subject*, by having willing originate entirely from the *subject* without making due allowance for the factor to be found in the *object*, namely the motives. These really determine the entirely individual nature of the actions, whereas only what is general and essential in them, namely their basic moral character, originates in the *subject*. However, such an inverted order which is natural to the understanding in speculative investigations should not surprise us, for originally the understanding is destined solely for practical and not at all for speculative purposes. –

Now if in consequence of the foregoing discussion we have entirely suspended from human action all freedom and have recognized that such action is thoroughly subject to the strictest necessity, we are thus led to the point where we shall be able to understand *true moral freedom*, which is of a higher kind.

For there is still a fact of consciousness which, to avoid disturbing the course of our investigation, I have so far entirely disregarded. This is the perfectly clear and certain feeling of *responsibility* for what we do, of *accountability* for our actions – a feeling that rests on the unshakable certainty that we ourselves are *the doers of our deeds*. On the strength of that consciousness, it never occurs to anyone, not even to someone who is fully convinced of the necessity (previously discussed) with which our actions occur, to make use of this necessity as an excuse for a

93

transgression, and to throw the blame on the motives because their appearance rendered the deed inevitable. For he sees quite well that this necessity has a *subjective* condition, and that here *objectively* it depended on the latter alone; in other words, in existing circumstances and hence under the influence of the motives that have determined him, an entirely different action, in fact the very opposite of his, was quite possible and could have happened, *if only he had been another person.* Because he is this person and not another; because he has such-and-such a character, naturally no other action was possible for *him*; in itself, however, and thus *objectively*, it is possible. Therefore the *responsibility* of which he is conscious concerns the deed only in the first instance and ostensibly, but at bottom it concerns *his character*; it is for the latter that he feels himself responsible. And for the latter he is also made responsible by others, since their judgment turns at once from the deed to ascertain the qualities of the doer. "He is a bad human being, a rogue," or "he is a scoundrel," or "he is a petty, false, mean 94 soul" – such is their verdict, and their reproaches recur to his *character.* The deed together with the motive is regarded here merely as evidence of the character of the doer; it is looked upon as a sure symptom of the character by which the latter is established irrevocably and for all time. Therefore Aristotle quite rightly says: Ἐγκωμιάζομεν πράξαντας. τὰ δ'ἔργα σημεῖα τῆς ἕξεώς ἐστι, ἐπεὶ ἐπαινοῖμεν ἂν καὶ μὴ πεπραγότα, εἰ πιστεύοιμεν εἶναι τοιοῦτον. *Rhetoric*, I, 9, 1367b 31. (*Encomio celebramus eos, qui egerunt: opera autem signa habitus sunt; quoniam laudaremus etiam qui non egisset, si crederemus esse talem.*)[3] Therefore hatred, loathing, and contempt are poured not on the passing deed but on the abiding qualities of the doer, i.e., of the character from which they have sprung. Hence in all languages the epithets of moral depravity, the terms of opprobrium which they express, are predicates of the *human being* rather than of the actions. They are attached to the *character*; for the latter must bear the guilt of which it has been convicted merely on the evidence of the deeds.

Where the *guilt* lies, there too must lie the *responsibility*; and as the latter is the sole datum that justifies the inference to moral freedom, so too must *freedom* lie in that very place, hence in the *character* of the

---

[3] "We praise those who have carried out an action, but actions are only an indication of the character. We would also award praise, even if the act were left undone, provided that we believed that the human being was capable of doing it."

human being; the more so, because we have sufficiently convinced ourselves that freedom is not to be met with directly in the individual actions, which, given the character, enter with strict necessity. But, as was shown in the third section, the character is inborn and unalterable.

Therefore we will now consider somewhat more closely freedom in this sense, the only one for which the data exist, in order to comprehend it philosophically, to the extent that this might be possible, after we have inferred it from a fact of consciousness and have found its place.

95 In the third section we saw that every action of a human being was the product of two factors, his character together with the motive. This certainly does not mean that the action is something intermediate, a compromise as it were between the motive and the character. On the contrary, the action entirely satisfies both, since it depends in its very possibility on both simultaneously, namely on the fact that the operating motive meets with this character, and that the latter is determinable by such a motive. The character is the empirically known, constant, and unalterable disposition of an individual will. Now as this character is just as necessary a factor of every action as is the motive, we thus have an explanation of the feeling that our deeds come from ourselves or of that "*I will*" which accompanies all our actions, and by virtue of which everyone must acknowledge them to be *his* deeds, for which he therefore feels himself morally responsible. Now this again is just the "I will, and will always only what I will" which we found previously in our investigation of self-consciousness, and which misleads the untutored understanding into obstinately asserting an absolute freedom of commission and omission, a *liberum arbitrium indifferentiae*. But it is nothing more than the consciousness of the second factor of the action, which by itself alone would be quite incapable of bringing about the action, but which, on the other hand, with the entrance of the motive is just as incapable of leaving the action undone. But only by being moved to activity in this way does the character reveal its own quality to the faculty of cognition, which, directed essentially outward and not inward as it is, first comes to know even the true nature of its own will empirically from the latter's actions. It is really this closer and ever more intimate acquaintance that is called *conscience*, which for this very reason first makes itself heard *directly only after* the actions; *prior to it* it announces itself at best only *indirectly*, since, as something occurring in

the future, it may be taken into account during deliberation by reflecting and looking back on similar cases about which it has already declared itself.

Now here is the place to remind the reader of the account, mentioned in the preceding section, which *Kant* gave of the relation between the empirical and intelligible character, and thus of the compatibility of freedom with necessity, which is one of the finest and profoundest creations of that great mind, indeed of all humankind. I need only refer to it, for to repeat it here would be lengthy and superfluous. But only from it can one understand, to the extent that human powers are capable of understanding this, how the strict necessity of our actions still coexists with that freedom to which the feeling of responsibility testifies and by virtue of which we are the doers of our deeds and these are attributable to us. – That relation, explained by *Kant*, between the empirical and intelligible character rests entirely on what constitutes the fundamental trait of his entire philosophy, namely the distinction between appearance and thing in itself; and as with him the complete *empirical reality* of the world of experience coexists with its *transcendental ideality*, so does the strict *empirical necessity* of acting coexist with its *transcendental freedom*. For the empirical character, like the whole human being, is as an object of experience a mere appearance, hence tied to the forms of all appearance, to time, space, and causality, and subject to their laws. On the other hand, the condition and basis of this whole appearance is the human being's *intelligible character*, i.e., his will as thing in itself, which is independent of those forms and therefore subject to no time distinction and consequently permanent and unchangeable, and to which certainly also belongs absolute freedom, i.e., independence from the law of causality (as a mere form of appearances). This freedom, however, is *transcendental*, i.e., it does not emerge in the appearance but is present only insofar as we abstract from the apprearance and all its forms in order to arrive at that which, outside all time, is to be thought of as the inner essence of the human being in himself. By virtue of this freedom, all deeds of a human being are his own work, however necessarily they may proceed from the empirical character when the latter meets with the motives. They are his own work because this empirical character is merely the appearance of the intelligible character in our *faculty of cognition* – a faculty that is bound to time, space, and causality. In other words, the empirical character is the mode and manner in which the very essence of our own self exhibits itself to the faculty of cognition. Consequently, the *will* is indeed free, but only in itself and outside the appearance. In the latter, on the other hand, it already manifests itself with a definite character to which all its deeds must conform, and consequently turn out necessarily *thus* and not otherwise when they are determined more specifically by the motives that enter.

It is easy to see that this path leads to our having to look for the work of our *freedom* no longer in our individual actions, as the common view does, but in the whole being and essence (*existentia et essentia*) of the human being himself, which must be conceived as his free act manifesting itself merely for the faculty of cognition (tied as the latter is to time, space, and causality) in a plurality and diversity of actions. But just because of the original unity of that which manifests itself in those actions, they must all bear exactly the same character, and therefore appear as strictly necessitated by the respective motives that produce them and determine them in the particular case. Accordingly, for the world of experience, the statement *operari sequitur esse* holds good without exception. Everything operates in accordance with its nature, and its acting, which follows from causes, proclaims that nature. Every human being acts in accordance with what he is, and the action, which is accordingly always necessary in each case, is determined in the individual case by the motives alone. *Freedom*, which therefore cannot be met with in the *operari*, *must lie in the esse*. It has been a fundamental error, a ὕστερον πρότερον[4] of all ages, to attribute necessity to the *esse* and freedom to the *operari*. On the contrary, *in the esse alone is freedom to be found*, but from the *esse* and the motives the *operari* necessarily follows, and *in what we do we recognize what we are*. On this, and not on the alleged *liberum arbitrium indifferentiae*, rest the awareness of responsibility and the moral tendency of life. It all depends on what someone *is*; what he *does* will automatically result from it as a necessary corollary. The consciousness of spontaneity and originality that undeniably accompanies all our deeds and by virtue of which they are *our* deeds, in spite of their dependence on the motives, is therefore not deceptive. Its content, however, extends beyond the deeds and originates higher up, since our being and essence themselves, from which all

---

[4] "Putting the later earlier."

98 deeds necessarily proceed (on the occasion of the motives), are really included in it. In this sense that consciousness of spontaneity and originality, as well as that of the responsibility accompanying our actions, can be compared to an indicator that points to an object more distant than the nearer one in the same direction to which it seems to point.

In a word, a human being always does only what he wills, and yet he necessarily does it. This is owing to the fact that he already *is* what he wills; for from what he is all that he ever does follows of necessity. If we consider his actions *objectively*, i.e., from without, we recognize apodictically that, like the actions of every being in nature, they must be subject to the law of causality in all its strictness. *Subjectively*, on the other hand, everyone feels that he always does only what he *wills*. But this means merely that his actions are the pure manifestation of his very own essence. Therefore if it could feel, every being in nature, even the lowest, would feel the same thing.

Freedom, then, is not suspended by my treatment of the matter, but merely moved up from the domain of individual actions, where it obviously is not to be found, into a higher region, which, however, is not so easily accessible to our cognition; in other words, freedom is transcendental. And this too is the sense in which I would like us to understand Malebranche's[5] saying, *la liberté est un mystère*,[6] under whose aegis the present treatise has attempted to solve the problem propounded by the Royal Society.

---

[5] Nicolas de Malebranche (1638–1715): French philosopher and Catholic priest.

[6] "Freedom is a mystery." This phrase, which also serves as the motto of Schopenhauer's *Prize Essay*, is a paraphrase rather than a quotation from Malebranche. See the introduction to the present edition.

Appendix
Supplementing the first section

In consequence of the division of freedom, given at the very beginning, into physical, intellectual, and moral, I have still to discuss the second after dealing with the first and third. This is done merely for the sake of completeness, so we can be brief.

The intellect or the faculty of cognition is the *medium of motives*. For through it motives act on the will, which is the real kernel of the human being. Only insofar as this medium of motives happens to be in a normal state or condition, fulfills its functions regularly, and thus presents to the will for choice the motives in an unfalsified manner as they exist in the real world can this will decide according to its nature, i.e., in accordance with the individual character of the human being, and thus manifest itself *unimpeded* in conformity with its very own essence. The human being is then *intellectually free*, i.e., his actions are the pure result of the reaction of his will to motives that lie in the outside world before him as also before everyone else. Consequently, those actions can be imputed to him morally as well as juridically.

This intellectual freedom is *suspended* either through the permanent or temporary derangement of the medium of motives, the faculty of cognition, or by a faulty apprehension of motives which is caused by external circumstances in the particular case. The former is the case in madness, delirium, paroxysm, and heavy drowsiness; the latter occurs when a decisive but innocent mistake has been made, e.g., when instead of medicine poison is administered, or a servant entering at night is mistaken for a burglar and shot, and so on. For in both cases the motives are falsified, and thus the will cannot decide as it would in the existing circumstances if the intellect correctly transmitted them to it.

Crimes committed in such circumstances are therefore not punishable by law. For laws start from the correct assumption that the will is not morally free, for otherwise it could not be *directed*, but that it is subject to compulsion by motives. Accordingly, the object of laws is to oppose all possible motives to crime by stronger countermotives in the form of threatened penalties, and a penal code is nothing but a catalog of countermotives to criminal actions. But if it is established that the intellect through which these countermotives had to act was incapable of apprehending them and presenting them to the will, then their effect was not possible; they did not exist for the will. It is as if we had found broken one of the ropes that had to move a machine. In such a case, therefore, the guilt passes from the will to the intellect; but the latter is subject to no penalty. On the contrary, laws, like morality, are concerned solely with the will. It alone is the real human being; the intellect is merely its organ, its outwardly directed antennae, i.e., the medium of the effect on it through motives.

100

Deeds of this kind are also just as little imputable from a *moral* point of view; for they are not traits of the human being's character. He has either done something different from what he imagined he was doing, or was incapable of thinking of what should have prevented him from doing it, i.e., of admitting the countermotives. Here it is as if a substance being examined chemically is exposed to the influence of several reagents so that one may see for which of these it has the strongest affinity. If after the experiment it is found that, through an accidental obstacle, one of the reagents could not exert its influence at all, then the experiment is null and void.

Intellectual freedom, here regarded as entirely suspended, can also be merely *diminished* or partially suspended. This occurs especially through affect and intoxication. *Affect* is the sudden, vehement stirring of the will through a representation forcing its way in from without and becoming the motive, which is so vivid that it obscures all others that could counteract it and prevents them from clearly entering consciousness. The countermotives are often only of an abstract nature, mere thoughts, whereas the motivating affection is something intuited, something that is present. The countermotives, so to speak, do not get a chance, and so do not have *fair play*, as they say in English; the deed has already been done before they could counteract. It is as if one of the parties in a duel fires before the word of command is given. Here, too, then juridical as well as moral responsibility is, by the nature of the circumstances, more or less, in any case partially, suspended. In England a murder committed in complete precipitance and without the least premeditation, in the most vehement and suddenly excited anger, is called *manslaughter*, and is punished lightly or sometimes not at all. – *Intoxication* is a state that predisposes to affects, since it enhances the vividness of the intuitive representations; on the other hand, it weakens abstract thinking and at the same time intensifies the energy of the will. Hence, in place of responsibility for the deeds, there is responsibility for the intoxication itself. Therefore intoxication is not excused juridically, although intellectual freedom is partially suspended here.

101

Aristotle speaks of this intellectual freedom, τὸ ἑκούσιον καὶ ἀκούσιον κατὰ διάνοιαν,[1] although very briefly and inadequately, in the *Eudemian Ethics*, II, 7 and 9, and in somewhat more detail in the *Nicomachean Ethics*, III, 2. – It is what is referred to when forensic medicine and criminal justice ask whether a criminal was in a state of freedom and consequently accountable for his actions.

In general, therefore, we may regard as committed in the absence of intellectual freedom all those crimes in which a human being either did not know what he was doing, or was absolutely incapable of taking into consideration what should have prevented him from so acting, namely the consequences of the deed. Accordingly, in such cases he cannot be punished.

Those, on the other hand, who are of the opinion that, because of the nonexistence of *moral* freedom and of the consequent inevitability of all the actions of a given human being, no criminal should be punished start from a false view of punishment. They think that it is a visitation of crimes for their own sake, a requital of evil with evil on moral grounds. But although this has been taught by *Kant*, such a thing would be absurd, purposeless, and absolutely unjustified. For how could a human being have the right to appoint himself as the absolute judge of another in a moral regard, and as such to torment him because of his sins! On the contrary, the law, i.e., the threat of punishment, aims at being the countermotive to crimes not yet committed. If in the particular case it fails to do this, the punishment must be carried out, since it would otherwise fail in all future cases. In this case, the criminal

---

[1] "The voluntary and involuntary with respect to thought."

on his part indeed undergoes the punishment in consequence of his moral nature, which, in conjunction with the circumstances that were the motives and his intellect that deceived him into hoping he would escape punishment, inevitably brought about the deed. Here an injustice could be done to him only if his moral character were not his own work, his intelligible deed, but the work of someone else. The same relation between the deed and its sequel occurs when the consequences of a human being's vicious conduct come about in accordance with natural and not human laws; e.g., when dissolute excesses produce terrible diseases, or when someone attempting to commit a burglary meets with an accident, e.g., when someone is breaking into a pigsty at night, in order to remove its usual inmates, and instead of these finds, coming toward him with open arms, a bear whose master is spending the night at that wayside inn.

102

Appendix
Eric F. J. Payne, translator
BRYAN MAGEE

With the publication of this volume Schopenhauer's whole significant output becomes available to English-language readers in a good and uniform translation. This monumental achievement is the work of E. F. J. Payne, who died on 12 January 1983 at the age of almost eighty-eight. He was not an academic but a professional soldier. His story is so unusual that it deserves telling for its own sake as well as in tribute to his achievement.

In 1907, when Eric Payne was twelve years old, his father became Secretary to the Buddhist Society of Great Britain and Ireland, and also Editor of the *Buddhist Review*. Father made no attempt to influence son, but the boy grew up in an atmosphere in which Buddhism was a familiar element, and was influenced nevertheless. He joined the British Army during the First World War, and stayed on afterward as a regular soldier. From 1920 to 1930 he was drafted to India – and there he became deeply and seriously involved in Buddhist studies.

On his return to England in 1930 his father gave him some of Schopenhauer's essays in an English translation by Bailey Saunders. These came to him as, in his own words, "a revelation." He went on to read the then-prevailing English translation, by Haldane and Kemp, of Schopenhauer's masterpiece *Die Welt als Wille und Vorstellung*. The experience bowled him over. Here was a philosopher in the mainstream of the Western tradition, steeped in the work of the greatest Western philosophers from Plato to Kant, not only knowledgeable about science but highly respectful of it as being central to man's attempt to understand himself and the world; and by traveling along these paths, none of which passed through India, he had found himself arriving at fundamental conclusions similar to those of Buddhism.

In a state of intellectual excitement Payne learnt German so as to be able to read Schopenhauer in the original. When he did so he was made aware of several shortcomings in the Haldane and Kemp translation. Alongside this he came to feel that all Schopenhauer's writings, not only his main work, ought to be made available to English-readers in accurate translations. However, he continued for many years to marinade in the originals without attempting to do anything about translating them – throughout the Second World War and another period of army service in India and the Far East. In 1947, by now a colonel, he was posted to Germany for his final tour of duty before retirement, and there he met the doyen of recent editors of Schopenhauer's work, Arthur Hübscher. With Hübscher's help and encouragement he embarked on what was to be his true life's work, the translation of all Schopenhauer's writings into English.

He began with *Die Welt als Wille und Vorstellung*. His translation of this was a many-sided improvement on that of Haldane and Kemp, but even so he had difficulty in finding a publisher for it. Eventually it was produced in two hardback volumes by the Falcon's Wing Press of Indian Hills, Colorado. But it soon went out of print and was unavailable again. Eventually the rights were taken over by Dover Publications of New York, who brought it out in two paperback volumes in 1966 and remains its present-day publisher.

By this time Payne was continuing to work on the translation of Schopenhauer's other writings. But publishers were even less enthusiastic about investing in the secondary works than they had been about investing in the primary one, and the rejections and disappointments piled up as Payne went on producing more and more translations. He did have one or two early successes, but there was a long period in his life when he had completed the translation of many volumes without any perceptible hope of their publication; and yet he was still working full-time at producing new ones, obscurely confident that somehow it would come right in the end. And somehow it did.

In the very long run the books found different homes with different publishers, several of them after Eric's death. To list them all, *On the Basis of Morality* was published first by Bobbs-Merrill and then by Berghahn Books; *On the Fourfold Root of the Principle of Sufficient*

Reason by Open Court Publishing Company; *Parerga and Paralipomena* (Schopenhauer's outstanding two-volume collection of essays) by Oxford University Press; *On the Will in Nature* by Berg, together with *On Vision and Colors* and all four volumes of Schopenhauer's posthumous writings under the title *Manuscript Remains*.

Having played a small role in bringing some of this about, I was made aware that a position had been reached in which all but one of Eric's translations had been published. The exception was the *Prize Essay on the Freedom of the Will*. But the manuscript, though known to exist, was nowhere to be found. Eric died at an advanced age and left everything to his wife, who then died and left everything to their only child, whose home was in Paris but who herself died, comparatively young, of cancer. I instigated a ransacking of forgotten papers in garrets and boxes in Paris, London, and the Sussex countryside. After much time and searching the manuscript was found. The published version of it is what the reader now holds in her hands.

By making Schopenhauer's entire output available to English-speakers with no German, and doing so in the teeth of literally decades of discouragement, Payne has performed a more heroic service for philosophy in the English-speaking world than anything he accomplished as a professional soldier. People nowadays are coming more and more to regard Schopenhauer as one of the truly great philosophers; and, this being so, more and more of them are finding themselves in Eric Payne's debt as the years go by. For this he deserves to be remembered. A short, stocky man with a squareish head and merry eyes, he surprisingly resembled certain portraits of Schopenhauer. Anyone who believes in reincarnation, as presumably all of Eric's Buddhist readers do, might be tempted to wonder . . . Those of us who do not noted the resemblance merely, and teased him about it. But, physical resemblance or no, there can be few individuals since Schopenhauer who have done so much for his philosophy.

Index

act, free, 87; *see also* will, act/acts of

action, 10, 17, 22, 34, 72, 83–7; accountability of, 83, 91; an animal's, 35; bad, 65–6; bodily, 14, 16; considered objectively, 88; considered subjectively, 88; deliberate and intentional, 31; human, 83; imputation of, 89; individual, 85, 87–8; individual nature of, 83; as manifestation of a human being's essence, 88; mode of, 51; moral worth of, 44; and reaction, 26

affect, 10, 58, 90–1

affections, 10–11

ancients, the, 47, 54, 57, 83

animal, 25, 27–8, 30–1, 34

animal functions, 28

animal life, 28, 34

appearance, 23, 29, 39, 86

apperception, 28

apprehension: intuitive, 20; of motives, 89; objective, 23; power of, 30

Apuleius, 46

Aristotle, 4, 47, 57–8, 84, 91

aseitas (aseity), 65–6

Augustine, 9 n. b, 10 n. c, 59–61, 63–4, 67

bad, evil and, 60

Bayle, Pierre, 52

being: and essence, 87; every, 88; whole, 87; a willing, 23

being, human, 25, 29–32, 34–40, 42–51, 65–6, 84–6, 88–92; essence of the, 86; experience of himself, 18; kernel of the, 89; ordinary, 18; relation to nature, 18; a practical and not a theoretical being, 16

body, 14, 26, 32; animal, 27; control over, 76; inanimate, 26, 35; inorganic, 25–6;

as organ of the will, 11; organic, 33; our, 11, 16

Böhme, Jakob, 75

brain, 28, 32

Buridan, John, 52–3, 67

caritas (Christian virtue of love), 47

causality, xviii, 8, 13, 31–2, 40–1, 86; *a priori* validity of, 25; forms of, 32; law of, 23–5, 39, 51, 86

causation, motivational, xviii

cause, xiv, 24–6, 29, 31–7, 39–42, 51, 58, 87; determining, 37, 40; effective, 35; external, 29, 31, 53; in general, 35, 40, 50; mechanical, 32, 40, 58; in the narrowest sense, 25–6, 32, 41–2; operating, 39; particular, 50

chain, causal, 54

chance, 49, 66

change, 24–6, 40

character, xxi, 44–5, 49–51, 53, 57, 82, 84–5, 87, 90; acquired, 43; another, 38; constant, 44; definite, 87; difference of, 48; of the doer, 84; empirical, 42–4, 72–4, 86–7; formation of the, 49; or heart, 45; hereditary, 46; inborn, 46, 50, 66, 85; individual, 20, 35, 42, 47, 50, 89; intelligible, 73–4, 86; moral, 83, 92; moral difference of, 42; original, 42; as a person's actual morality, 46; of the species, 42; unalterable, 46, 54, 85

choice, 30–1, 34, 42–3, 89; objects of, 17

Chrysippus, 58

Cicero, 9 n. b, 58

Clement of Alexandria, 58

cognition, xix, 27–8, 43, 45–6, 49; *a priori*, 18; external, 34; faculty of, 8–9, 12, 15, 22–4, 40, 85–7, 89; forms of, 8; ground of, 24; internal, 34; as medium of causality, 41;

97

cognition (*cont.*)
    as medium of the motives, 45; metaphysical, 82; nonintuitive, 35; object(s) of, 40, 77; of the understanding, 19
common sense: ordinary, 20, 83; sound, 5; untutored, 83
complex, conceptual, 30
concepts, 29–30, 35; abstract, 30; universal, 29
Condillac, Etienne Bonnot de, 76
conduct, irrational and rational, 30
connection, causal, 40
conscience 45, 85
conscientia (conscience), 9
consciousness, xv, 28, 34, 85; animal, 29; fact of, 38, 83, 85; ground of, 18; human, 29; immediate, 16; of other things, 8–9, 11, 14, 22–3; rational, 35; of responsibility, 83–4, 88; sensuous, 29; of spontaneity and originality, 87–8; total, 19; *see also* self-consciousness
contingent, 7; absolutely, 7, 40; relatively, 7
conviction, moral, 49
counteraction, 26
countermotive, 5, 36, 38, 90–1; *see also* motive
Cousin, Victor, 38, 76
Creator, the, 65–6
crime, 90–1

Dante, 52, 67
death, fear of, 38
decision, 10, 15–16, 32
deed, 10, 14, 38, 42, 44, 50, 54, 57, 83–7, 90–1; intelligible, 92
deliberation, 31–2
Descartes, René, 10 n. b, 12–13
difference, moral, 49
Diodorus, 58
doing, 20

education, moral and religious, 9
effect, 23–7, 31–5, 38, 40–2, 50; *see also* cause
efficacy, 36, 40; mode of, 28
ens metaphysicum (metaphysical being), 51
Erdmann, Johann Eduard, 74
essence, 51, 88–9; pure manifestations of, 88
essentia (essence), 51, 65, 87
evil: and bad, 60; good and, 75; requital of, 91
existentia (existence), 51, 65, 87
experience, 9, 18–19, 23–5; external, 25; objects of, 23, 25–6, 39; possibility of, 24–5; possible, 25
explanation, 41

fatum (fate), 54

feelings, inner, 19
Fichte, Johann Gottlieb, 74–5
force, xxi, 13, 40; manifestation(s) of, 28, 41, 50–1; moving, 28; natural, 29, 50; of nature, 41–2; original, 40–1; vital, 27, 29, 41–2, 51
free, 3, 6–8, 16, 77; comparatively, 64; meaning "in conformity with one's own will," 5; intellectually, 89; morally 90; relatively, 31; that which is in no relation necessary, 7; and voluntary, 57, 60; *see also* act, free; will, free
freedom, xii; absolute, 32, 54, 85–6; abstract sense of, 12; of acting, 5; comparative, 31–2; compatibility with necessity, 73, 86; of doing, 14; empirical concept of, 6; in the *esse*, 87; human, 73; intellectual, 4, 54, 89–91; Kant's moral proof or rather postulate of, 9; moral, 3–4, 57, 76–7, 84, 91; negative, 3, 66; in the *operari*, 87; original concept of, 6; popular concept of, 5, 14; physical, 3–4, 20, 57, 90; political, 4; relative, 31, 32; in Schelling, 75; state of, 91; transcendental, 86, 88; true moral, 83; to will or not to will, 12; of the will, 14, 38, 39; of the will itself, 5; of willing, 5, 6; *see also* will, freedom of the
future: foreseeing the, 54; objectively real, 54

geometry, 24
Goethe, Johann Wolfgang von, xi, 50, 75, 79
good, and evil, 75
ground: and consequent, 7; logical, 6; mathematical, 6; physical (i.e., causal), 6; sufficient, 6–7
guilt, 65–6, 85, 90

head, 45
Hegel, Friedrich Georg Wilhelm, ix, xi n. 7, 76
Herodotus, 43
Hobbes, Thomas, 48 n. d, 67–8
Hume, David, 63, 69

"I will," the, which accompanies all our actions, 22, 85
ideal, the, relation to the real, 57, 83
idealism, xxiv, 74
ideality, transcendental, 86
identity, principle of, 17
imagination, 37
imperatives, categorical, 9
impression, 30–2
inclination, 66
individual, 66
inexplicable, the, 29, 41
intellect, 13, 27, 89–91; *see also* understanding
intelligence, human, 36

intuition, 9, 16, 19, 23, 29–31; sensible, 30; world of sensible, 16

judgment, 40
justice, forensic and criminal, 91

Kant, Immanuel, x, 7, 9, 21, 24, 29, 38, 51, 64, 72–6, 82–3, 86, 91
knowing, 83
knowledge: of human beings, 44; problems of, 82; sphere of, 82

law, 90, 91; moral, 9; universal, 19
Leibniz, Gottfried Wilhelm, 13, 53
liberum arbitrium (free choice of the will), 3, 5, 21, 52, 64
liberum arbitrium indifferentiae (free choice of indifference), 8, 32, 35, 40, 49, 76–7, 85, 87
life, 27–8, 33; desire for, 38; moral tendency of, 87
Locke, John, xxiv, 10 n. b, 48, 76, 83
logic, 19, 49, 77
Lucian, 58
Luther, Martin, 56, 58, 60, 63

Malebranche, Nicolas de, xxix, 88
Manichaeans, 60, 67
mathematics, 19
merit, 65
metaphysics, 82
Mohammedans, 54
morals, 49
motion, 29, 35, 40
motivation, 25, 27, 29, 40–1; mode of, 31
motive(s), xxi, 5, 12–14, 28–44, 46, 50, 52–3, 66, 72, 82, 84–5, 87–91; abstract, 31–2, 36; causality of the, 30; conflict of, 32; intellect as medium of, 89; intuitive, 30, 31, 32; mutually exclusive, 37; opposing, 38; origin of, 35; *see also* countermotive
movement, 27–8

nature: human, 9; laws of, 36, 72; whole of, 39
necessary: is being the consequence/consequent of a given sufficient ground, 7, 24; is that which follows from a given sufficient ground, 6; and the voluntary, 58
necessity, 6–8, 11–13, 25, 32–3, 45, 50–5, 72, 84, 87–8; according to law, 15; of acts of will, 52, 70; of all that happens, 54–5; of causal connection, 40; of causal relation, 34; causality entails, 31; character of, 24; coexistence of freedom with, 73; compatibility of freedom with, 73, 86; complete, 32; concept of 13; of the effect(s),

31, 50; of the efficacy of abstract motives, 36; empirical, 86; inevitable, 63; logical, 6; mathematical, 6; negation of, 12; of our actions, 83; physical (i.e., causal), 6; physical and real, 7; for salvation, 59; strict, 53–4, 82–3, 85–6; without, 7
Nemesius, 59
nervous system, 28
Newton, Isaac, 26

object(s), 49, 83; animate, 25; external, 11; inorganic, 25; as motive, 12; organic, 25; real, 24–5, 31; in space, 24; of willing, 14; world of, 15
objective, the, 49; *see also* subjective, the
On the Fourfold Root of the Principle of Sufficient Reason, xiv–xv, 7 n. a, 24 n. a
On the Will in Nature, 33 n. c
operari sequitur esse (doing follows being), xxiii, 51, 65, 87
organism, 27

Parerga and Paralipomena, 15 n. a, 45
passions, 10, 58
Pelagians, 67
Pelagius, 59, 60
penalty, 90
phenomena, 41
philosopher, as opposed to naive human being, 16, 18
philosophers: alleged, 58; scholastic, 46, 51, 67
philosophy, modern, two problems of, xxiv, 57, 83
place, 31
plant, 25, 27, 29
plant life, 28
Plato, 53
poet(s), 45, 78, 81
possibility, subjective and objective, 15
power: cognitive, 14, 19; mental, 27; to act, 29
predestination, 54, 67
Priestley, Joseph, 48, 70–1
Prize Essay on the Freedom of the Will: organization of, xi–xii; origin of, ix; editions of, xxxv
punishment, 91

real, the, relation to the ideal, 57, 83
reality, 51; empirical, 86; of the external world, 57
reason, 29, 58; faculty of, 14, 18, 21; practical, 9; sufficient, principle of, 24, 40
reflecting, 31
reflection, 9, 37

relation, causal, 14, 20, 34
representations, 28; faculty of, 28; intuitive, 30, 34–5, 91; nonintuitive, 29–30
responsibility, 84; awareness of, 87; feeling of, 83, 86; juridical, 91; moral, 4, 91
Rousseau, Jean-Jacques, 45

Schelling, Friedrich Wilhelm Joseph, xi n. 7, 48, 74–5
Schiller, Friedrich, 77, 79
Schopenhauer, Arthur: anonymous reference to himself, 29; sketch of his life, x–xi
science, natural, 19
Scott, Walter, 78
self: own, 10, 87; real, 18
self-consciousness, xv, 8–22, 28–9, 76, 81, 85; the "I can *do* what I *will*" of, 38; immediate, 10–14, 18–19, 21; natural, 17; the only object of, 11; organ of, 10; simple, 72; statement of (viz., "I can do what I will"), 12, 20, 36; wrongly interpreted, 37; *see also* consciousness
Seneca, 48
sensation, 19
sense, inner, 9, 11, 19, 23
sense organ, 23
senses, 35; outer, 23
Shakespeare, William, 45, 78
sight, second, 54
sin, 65–6; original, 59, 67
Socrates, 47, 53, 57
somnambulism, 54
space, 8, 30–1, 86; as *a priori* intuited, 24
species, human, 29
Spinoza, Baruch, 65, 68–9, 71
spirit, 77–8
stimulus, 25–8, 32–5, 41–2
subject, 83; that wills, 58
subjective, the, 49; *see also* objective, the

thing in itself, x, 29, 86
think, ability to, 31
thinking, 9, 29; abstract, 91; faculty of, 19
thought, 30–1, 35–6, 39
time, 8, 30–1, 86

truths: concatenation of, 82; negative *a priori*, 21

understanding, 23, 34, 40, 49–50, 83; cognition of the, 19; human 35; practical destination of, 83; pure, 14, 21, 36, 39; universal rules of, 18; untutored, 49, 85; *see also* intellect
unity, original, 87
uinwillingness, feeling of, 10

Vanini, Lucilio, 62–3
velleitas (wish), 37
Velleius Paterculus, 48
virtue and vice, 47–8
Voltaire, 71
voluntary, 3, 57, 60
voluntas (will), 37

will, xix, 10–11, 34, 42–3, 51, 65, 89–90; act/acts of, 10–16, 18, 20, 52; affections of the, 10–11; of animals 3–4; beings endowed with a, 23; consequences of, 17; determining ground of the, 28–9; energy of the, 91; as force, 41; free, 8, 59–60, 65–7, 87; freedom of our, 36; freedom of the, 8–9, 11, 14, 16, 20, 38–40, 43, 48–9, 51, 53, 57–60, 66, 76, 83; freedom of the human, 3; grounds of the, 17; of a human being, 7, 18, 46, 51; individual, 7, 85; as inner moving force, 28; inner perception of the, 19, 73; manifestations of the, 7–8; movements of the, 11; opposite acts of, 15; organ of the, 11; outer perception of the, 73; as *tabula rasa*, 65; *see also* act, free; free; freedom
willing, xvii, 17, 20, 83; determining grounds for the, 15; manifestations of, 10; and not-willing, 11, 19; objects of, 14; the opposite, 20; of his willing, 17; presupposition of, 14
wishing, as opposed to willing, xvii, 15
words, used to fix universal concepts, 29
world: external, 11, 19, 22–3; inner and outer, 16; of intuition, 16; material, 24; objective, 24; real, 7, 24, 89; real external, 23; real outer, 9; of thought/thoughts, 19, 24
World as Will and Representation, The, ix, 30

Cambridge texts in the history of philosophy

Titles published in the series thus far

Antoine Arnauld and Pierre Nicole *Logic or the Art of Thinking* (edited by Jill Vance Buroker)

Boyle *A Free Enquiry into the Vulgarly Received Notion of Nature* (edited by Edward B. Davis and Michael Hunter)

Bruno *Cause, Principle and Unity* and *Essays on Magic* (edited by Richard Blackwell and Robert de Lucca with an introduction by Alfonso Ingegno)

Clarke *A Demonstration of the Being and Attributes of God and Other Writings* (edited by Ezio Vailati)

Conway *The Principles of the Most Ancient and Modern Philosophy* (edited by Allison P. Coudert and Taylor Corse)

Cudworth *A Treatise Concerning Eternal and Immutable Morality* with *A Treatise of Freewill* (edited by Sarah Hutton)

Descartes *Meditations on First Philosophy*, with selections from the *Objections and Replies* (edited with an introduction by John Cottingham)

Descartes *The World and Other Writings* (edited by Stephen Gaukroger)

Hobbes and Bramhall on Liberty and Necessity (edited by Vere Chappell)

Kant *Critique of Practical Reason* (edited by Mary Gregor with an introduction by Andrews Reath)

Kant *Groundwork of the Metaphysics of Morals* (edited by Mary Gregor with an introduction by Christine M. Korsgaard)

Kant *The Metaphysics of Morals* (edited by Mary Gregor with an introduction by Roger Sullivan)

Kant *Prolegomena to Any Future Metaphysics* (edited by Gary Hatfield)

Kant *Religion within the Boundaries of Mere Reason and Other Writings* (edited by Allen Wood and George di Giovanni with an introduction by Robert Merrihew Adams)

La Mettrie *Machine Man and Other Writings* (edited by Ann Thomson)

Leibniz *New Essays on Human Understanding* (edited by Peter Remnant and Jonathan Bennett)

Malebranche *Dialogues on Metaphysics and on Religion* (edited by Nicholas Jolley and David Scott)

Malebranche *The Search after Truth* (edited by Thomas M. Lennon and Paul J. Olscamp)

Melanchthon *Orations on Philosophy and Education* (edited by Sachiko Kusukawa and Christine Salazar)

Mendelssohn *Philosophical Writings* (edited by Daniel O. Dahlstrom)

Nietzsche, *The Birth of Tragedy and Other Writings* (edited by Raymond Geuss and Ronald Speirs)

Nietzsche *Daybreak* (edited by Maudemarie Clark and Brian Leiter, translated by R. J. Hollingdale)

Nietzsche *Human, All Too Human* (translated by R. J. Hollingdale with an introduction by Richard Schacht)
Nietzsche *Untimely Meditations* (edited by Daniel Breazeale, translated by R. J. Hollingdale)
Schleiermacher *Hermeneutics and Criticism* (edited by Andrew Bowie)
Schleiermacher *On Religion: Speeches to its Cultured Despisers* (edited by Richard Crouter)
Schopenhauer *Prize Essay on the Freedom of the Will* (edited by Günter Zöller)